P9-CRN-984

"Octavio Solis does with words and imagery, lyricism and details, humor and heartbreak what the master craftsmen and women of the traditional *retablos* do with wood and paint, achieving the same results: these short luminous *retablos* are magical and enticing. Unpretentiously and with an unerring accuracy of tone and rhythm, Solis slowly builds what amounts to a storybook cathedral. We inhabit a border world rich in characters, lush with details, playful and poignant, a border that refutes the stereotypes and divisions smaller minds create. Solis reminds us that sometimes the most profound truths are best told with crafted fictions—and he is a master at it. His is a large, capacious, and inclusive imagination. Just as the traditional *retablos* are objects of beauty ultimately meant as devotional pieces, Solis's *Retablos* will make devotees of his readers."

—**Julia Alvarez** is the author of numerous books, including *How the García Girls Lost Their Accents*, and recipient of the National Medal for the Arts

"The murky flow of the Rio Grande River, the border patrol we call *la migra*, demons, a petty crime of stolen candy, street urchins, family squabbles, eccentric neighbors, and bike rides in which dust envelops a skinny kid named Octavio Solis. When he stops pedaling years later, he'll spank the dust from his clothes, but not all of it. Some of it clings to his very soul, and will cling to us, the readers, in this tender and perceptive memoir. This is American *and* Mexican literature a stone's throw from the always hustling El Paso border."

—**Gary Soto**, author of *The Elements of San Joaquin*

"Octavio Solis isn't a painter, but he ought to be. He's not a poet, but he could be. His isn't fiction or memoir but, like dreams, might be either. His vision of El Paso and the border is as though through an undulating haze of desert heat."

—**Dagoberto Gilb**, author of *Before the End, After the Beginning: Stories*

"Solis has written beautifully about his youth on the border, never flinching from his childish blunders, nor failing to find soul in the frailties of others. These stories soar and shimmer with poetry and a playwright's gift for dramatic compression, comedy and pathos running through them arm in arm. *Retablos* is deeply moving, and a joy."
—**Elizabeth McKenzie,** author of *The Portable Veblen: A Novel*

"To enter into this book is like walking into a shrine, walls lined with beautiful paintings, each one colorful and visceral, depicting memories, life on the border, death and sadness and joy. This is one of the most memorable books written about the borderlands in years. Solis writes, 'every memory we have has a patina of invention to it.' These stories have layer upon layer of images, meaning, and grace. Each short piece, each of the *'retablos'* is a stunning, masterful painting. Some you will want to stand in front of for a long time, and others are brilliantly uncomfortable and can make you weep if you linger too long."
—**Daniel Chacón,** author of *Hotel Juárez: Stories, Rooms and Loops*

"The short-short format is often called flash fiction these days, but Octavio Solis's stories are more like slow fiction: a moment unfolds, revealing a life, a way of life, generations. He explores the borderlands, not just the streets of El Paso where he grew up, just across the Rio Grande from Mexico, but also those liminal zones between fiction and nonfiction, childhood and adulthood, and magic and melancholy. Small but mighty, these stories will stay with you long after the moment has passed."
—**Frances Lefkowitz**, author of *To Have Not: A Memoir*

"A *retablo* is a devotional painting, playwright Octavio Solis tells us. In this poignantly written, heart-warming coming-of-age memoir, Solis pays tribute to those cornerstone moments in his life, negotiating borders at once personal and cultural, with such color that the reader is left spellbound. Astonishing, what more can I say?"
—**Greg Sarris**, author of *How a Mountain Was Made: Stories*

RETABLOS

STORIES FROM A LIFE LIVED ALONG THE BORDER

Octavio Solis

City Lights Books | San Francisco

Copyright © 2018 by Octavio Solis
All rights reserved

Cover and book design by Linda Ronan

Some of the stories in this book were previously printed in the following journals:

"Retablos," "Bad Blood," "The Sister," "Keening," "The Cotton," "Tumble-Down," and "My Right Foot" under the single title "Retablos" in *Zzyzzyva*, Winter Issue 102.

"Wild Kingdom" and "World Goes Away" in *Zzyzzyva*, Winter Issue 108.

"The Want" and "El Segundo" in *Huizache: The Magazine of Latino Literature*, Issue No. 6

"La Migra," "Siren Songs," "Red," "Nothing Happens," and "Neto" in *Arroyo Literary Review*, Spring 2017.

Library of Congress Cataloging-in-Publication Data
Names: Solis, Octavio, author.
Title: *Retablos* : stories from a life lived along the border / Octavio Solis.
 Other titles: Stories from a life lived along the border
 Description: San Francisco : City Lights Books, 2018. | "These retablos are true stories, but they're filled with lies. The core events are real, they happened, but the images on the peripheries which were faint to my view have been elaborated on . . ." — Page).
 Identifiers: LCCN 2018023444 (print) | LCCN 2018029844 (ebook) | ISBN   9780872867888 | ISBN 9780872867864
 Subjects: LCSH: Solis, Octavio—Childhood and youth. | Mexican American   authors—Biography. | Dramatists, American—Biography. | Authors,   American—Biography. | Mexican-American Border Region—Social conditions.
 Classification: LCC PS3569.O5572 (ebook) | LCC PS3569.O5572 Z46 2018 (print)
 | DDC 812/.54 [B] —dc23
 LC record available at https://lccn.loc.gov/2018023444

City Lights Books are published at the City Lights Bookstore
261 Columbus Avenue, San Francisco, CA 94133
www.citylights.com

For my father and mother, who bravely
undertook the life of every immigrant family
in America and by doing so, changed it.

Contents

ON MY "*RETABLOS*"

MEMORY IS ITS OWN MUSE. Every time we recall a specific moment in our past, we remember it differently; we embellish upon it, we turn it into a story or a fable, something that will draw a straighter line between the person we were then and who we are now. Consciously or unconsciously, we trim away the details that seem inconsequential in order to endow the things we remember with greater clarity, with even more weight and significance. And we make connections we weren't capable of noting before, so that each event in our past is seen in the context of other trials and rites and moments of insight. Sometimes, the spark of a single memory will ignite others, things we hadn't recalled until now, like suddenly realizing that the room we thought we knew so well has an extra door we never noticed before. Open that door and there's a new room with new its own store of memories.

This means that every memory has a patina of invention on it. That patina thickens every time we revisit those moments in our past, until they seem more like stories and myths of our formation, more dreamlike and yet more real than what really happened to us. So where is the fact of what actually happened? It's still there, lost inside of and enhanced by fiction.

When my memories of the actual events of my youth began to feel more like something I'd dreamed, I knew I had to write them down. By committing them to words on paper, I was reclaiming them as my own authentic recollections. But as the act of writing is inherently a fictive one, I found that

9

even the most authentic memory became imbued with the same strange unreality. I wondered if perhaps it wasn't actually my perspective, but something about the place I'd grown up, Texas, the border, *la frontera*, that was surreal. Some years ago, a substantial amount of naturally occurring lithium was discovered in El Paso's drinking water supply. Maybe that's what gives this otherworldly cast to my memories of the city of my origin, but I suggest it's more than that. I feel it's something verging on the divine, though not the divine we are taught to believe in.

That's why I choose to call these stories *retablos*. A *retablo* is a devotional painting, usually laid on a small, thin plate of cheap, repurposed metal, in which a dire event is depicted — an accident, a crime, an illness, a calamity, some terrible rift in a person's life, which they survive thanks to the intercession of the Divine. They are *ex-voto*, that is, "from a vow," commissioned and created as a form of thanks. At once visual and literary, they record the crisis, the divine mediation and the offering of thanks in a single frame, thus forming a kind of flash-fiction account of an electrifying, life-altering event. I imagined the stories of this collection in this same disconnected (and yet thoroughly interconnected) way.

I've found that every time I read one of the stories, the same thing happens. I change it a little, adding another patina, another layer to the memory. But this is what any writer should do in the interest of storytelling. In the end, they're only stories. I'm not interested in autobiography. If this is a memoir, it's a faulty one, because I have given myself leave to invent elements within it. I suppose I am using the poetic voice to convey the authentic. I am more interested in depicting the events of my life as a means to identify and limn the mythology of being brown along the US/Mexico border during a specific period in time, beyond politics, beyond polemics and rhetoric, in order to share those resonances with others who are my age and others who are experiencing similar things right now.

One thing I have learned from writing these *retablos*: the shit on the border never changes. There will always be those who want to come across, and those who want to keep them where they are. The push and pull, the friction between the tectonic plates that are Mexico and the US will always create mountains of stress, dislocation and upheaval among the people who live there. Maybe this is political, after all, but I think it's really a condition of our culture: it's how we live now, it is our particular mythology, replete with gods and monsters, heroes and fallen angels, troubadours and exiles.

In the end, I'm trying to figure myself out. I'm coming to terms with who I am by looking back at what I was. I wrote *Retablos* to see how that skinny brown kid riding his bike out there in the desert made sense of his complicated, deeply beautiful and troubled world. So that perhaps I might learn to make sense of the one I live in today.

RETABLOS

RETABLOS

THIS IS ME IN MY old room, unpacking my bags on the bed I slept in more than thirty years ago, hearing my mother titter at something on the TV while my dad is stirring the *caldo de pollo* on the stove. He blurts out something crude in Spanish and now both of them are roaring big as life, filling the house with horsey laughter. Then it hits me. This is how one of them will cry when the other dies.

I look out the window and I'm thirteen all over again, getting ready for school. A polar front blew all the way down from Canada and locked us in an overnight freeze and didn't even have the manners to leave us any snow. Just a chill air and ice on the power lines. But as I come down the hall for my breakfast, I see my sister standing outside the maid's room, snarling something to herself. I ask her what happened and she says, The birds are dead. What? The birds are dead, she says again. I look in the room and I see the maid, this young Mexican girl of twenty we hired to watch the house and cook food for us while my parents are at work, I see her sitting on her bed with her face in her hands. Sobs and the words *perdón, perdón* are slipping through her fingers. While she wipes her snot on her sleeve, I look past her at the cage where my mom's canaries are supposed to be perched. But they're not there. I come closer and find them both balled up and lifeless on the newspaper floor of the cage. They were old, their yellow feathers faded white, inherited from my grandmother when she moved to Fresno, only now they are dead. My sister says the maid left the window open and they froze.

They couldn't take the cold. She should've known. Now look at them, she says. I'm about to ask where Mom and Dad are, but then I hear them laughing in their room. Why would they be laughing? I cross the hall and open the door, which is weird 'cause they hardly ever close the door in the morning once they're up, and there they are, sitting on the bed next to each other, hands on their brows, crying so boisterously it sounds like they're busting at the seams at some practical joke. It's unnerving. I've never seen them wailing like this, bent over and shaking, their mouths contorted, bawling like children. I've seen my mom cry a few times, but never like this, and never my dad, who's not the kind of man inclined to such displays of emotion. For a pair of old birds, no less. There's something ancient about the way their wails change them, even give the room a different light. I think this is a holy moment and close the door and leave them to their searing sacred laughter.

That's how they come, these memories. Like a set of *retablos*, votive images painted on old beaten tin, marked with the mystery of being, with acts of transgression recorded for those who need to remember. That's what revisiting El Paso is like for me. Like walking into a retablo with a rusty surface for a sky, and misremembered family and friends for saints and supplicants and the lost distilled moments of my border past for miracles. They come to me at the strangest times, as if to remind me that I have lived this much because of them.

THE WAY OVER

Tenemos que ir, she says.
Aquí es donde vivo. Allá no, he says.
Pero allá es donde todos podemos vivir. Tú. Yo. Y el niño.
El niño.
Tenemos que pensar por el niño.

BUT THEY ARE *NIÑOS* THEMSELVES. Too young to get married, according to my grandmother Mamá Concha, who despises my sullen young father. Now that her daughter of sixteen is pregnant with me, she hates him even more. She beats him with her fists and kicks him in the shins whenever he comes by. But they're in love and the birth is near. So, what can she do? Mamá Concha gives her blessing, but on the condition that they move to *el Norte. Mis nietos* will be American, she says. She is newly married herself and has a room secured for them in the same tenement she lives in. So, in short order, they exchange vows and countries in an old church in El Paso.

Thus begins our America myth: three of us, my mother, father and me, crowded in a dingy tenement room with a hot plate to cook all the food. Mamá Concha and her new man two doors down. Community bath at the end of the hall. My mother and her mother have *pasaportes locales* which make them resident aliens and I'm a born citizen. My father, however, has none of his papers. He works in Juárez in an entry-level job in a bank, where he counts out crisp new bills of Mexican currency. When he moves to El Paso he loses the job but soon gets another selling ad space in Juárez for a radio station. Every morning he walks across the Santa Fe Bridge to work, then returns in the evening over the same span. Some months later, the officer at the checkpoint remembers him.

I see you come and go every day. What's going on with you?

I live here but I work there, my father says in that gruff voice that makes the facts facts.

Well, you can't do that, says the officer. A man lives where he works. If you want to cross, go ahead, but you won't be coming back in. Make up your mind where you want to live.

My wife is here. My baby is here.

So from now on, here is where you work. That is that.

Now he has to find a job in a city that speaks English. But he can't because he doesn't. With his limited language, he is good only for menial work. He washes dishes in a greasy burger and menudo diner on the worst shift possible, the grim overnight hours before dawn. But the cook likes him, he's good to him and teaches him how to make things on the grill because he needs someone to cover for him on the days when he will be too drunk or hungover to come to work. That's how my father becomes a short-order cook. One of the best in the city. It's what he will do for most of his life. For the sake and welfare of this *niño* and the four more who come later.

My mother. She's close to her Mamá Concha. With shared unspoken troubles, they work together cleaning the houses of rich people. It's hard with the children. One of whom dies. Even I almost lose it when I drink a bottle of turpentine left uncapped in a room being painted. My father runs all the way to the hospital with me turning white in his arms. My mother prays over and over, *Madre Santa*, don't make me bury another. My stomach is pumped, and I live.

Later, Immigration men come to the door. They have reports that an illegal is living in this residence. My mother says, please don't take my husband. I need him to watch my babies while I go to work. The men are embarrassed by their duty, and one of them gives my mother the name of an official in the INS. See him as soon as you can. He will make your man legal. Then they drive away with my father in their car. My mother rushes to the County Courthouse and finds this official after a long search. He listens to this pleading young mother with two children and one on the way and somehow grants her wish. Her husband will get his papers. This is a different time from now. A time when people know compassion. A time when kindness is haphazardly bestowed.

My father spends five days and nights with other deportees in a dank, joyless pen called *el corralón*. They are the blackest hours of his life. He cannot sleep. The place has a foul odor. Everyone around him looks as shamed as he feels. I'm not like them, he thinks. He wonders if he will be taken back across. Once he wanted that; once he yearned to return to the life he knew. But now he yearns only for his family. His one-room tenement home.

My mother gets him released after showing his proof of employment. They have procedures to perform to make him a resident, procedures that will allow him to live and work and pay taxes in a country that speaks English. In a way, what enables this to happen is me. My parents are legal and living in this country because of my brothers and sister and me. Decades will pass before they take a test and recite the oath of allegiance in English as fluently as anyone in this country, with their hands over their hearts as they become full, incontestable citizens.

I am an anchor baby. Someone coined the term to impugn the motives of immigrants coming to this country. They use it to suggest that for some couples conceiving a child is not an act of love but a ploy to secure the rights of residence. But every baby is an anchor for young parents navigating the stormy waters of daily life; every baby is an anchor for those who are looking for their true north, their purpose, their identity. We give our parents hope when they drift from bad times to bad times to worse. We give them solace when they consider going back to the little they had before. I anchor them to a place and an ideal worth living for. As they anchor me.

We have to go, *dice ella*.
Here is where I live. Not there, *dice él*.
But there is where we can all live. You. Me. And the child.
The child.
We have to think of the child.

IN THE SHIMMER

IN THE CLOUDED WINDOW OF my early childhood, I see my grand-mother. Mamá Concha we call her. She's undoing hair rollers and applying bright red lipstick before the bathroom mirror. I see her short stocky legs in their saggy hose slip into her shoes with the blocky heels. Her purse is redolent with the fragrance of Wrigley's Chewing Gum and scented tissues that seem to burst from inside every time she unclasps it. She gives me half a stick of spearmint, slipping the other half in her mouth. She dresses me up in my best shirt and pants and combs my hair till it's waxed down like Alfalfa's from the Our Gang serials. Then we're outside.

She's sitting beside me on the city bus noisily taking us downtown. I watch her nervous hands smooth the pinstripes of her blue cotton dress over and over while she smacks the gum in her mouth and stares straight ahead like a lover on her way to an assignation. The bus driver asks her something in Spanish and she answers in the old country manner.

Ay.

I catch his gaze through the mirror over his head, how his eyes probe and ponder over us during the whole length of the ride. She takes a tissue from her purse and with a little spit on it wipes the scuff off my shoes, which dangle just off the seat, and she tightens my laces till my feet throb. I hear the gassy exhalation of the bus heaving to a stop and the door swish-ing open to *La Placita de los Lagartos*, which is teeming with more people than I've ever seen in my life. The sun is high and bright. The tightness of her grip on my hand turns my fingers red as she guides us to the central fountain in the tree-lined plaza, where she lifts me up with her firm arms to her bosom and shows me the alligators basking in the radiant heat. One of them is dozing in its pond, and one has its jaws wide open, a soft-serve ice cream cone melting on its back. I count the cigarette butts and candy wrappers floating in the pond all around them. Is this what we came to see? No, not this.

More people gather in the plaza and in the windows of the buildings around us for a view of something to come. Is it a parade? Are we here for a parade? Above me the sky is a brilliant, unsullied blue so wide and cloudless and perfect, I could fall into it. My grandmother clamps my hand in hers and pushes through the murmuring mass of people. She's smaller than most of them, but with her purse she clears a path toward the street. Some give her the stink-eye, some jab their elbows back and sneer at me, but she doggedly charges on.

Then I lose her. Somehow, our knotted fingers come undone and I am set loose in the tangled forest of legs, shoes and handbags and even a little weenie dog on a leash, panting with fear and heat and congestion, and I think I must have the same look as I call out for her. Mamá Concha! Mamá Concha! I feel the crowd surge in one direction and knock me down and some lady's heel stamps on my hand and I start to cry. The sound of several cars coming to a stop somewhere nearby sets off a riotous noise that drowns out my cries. Shifting bodies pressed hard against each other toss me about like a *piñata*. I look straight up for even a fragment of that blue sky but now it's a swarm of balloons and millions of tiny shreds of colored paper flitting and falling like snowflakes on everyone. This clamor of the crowd, the yelling and whistling, I feel it in my teeth, my bones, all the way down to my feet, till the ground is bellowing against the weight of all the stomping, pounding, jerking feet. The storm of people is so consuming and suffocating, and it moves with such a single anarchic mind, that I think I'll drown in it, I think I'll die. I scream with all my strength, MAMÁ CONCHA! But I can't hear myself. I can't hear anything but this crazed thunder of voices.

Through a seam in the wall of bodies, the hands of my grandmother emerge and take me by the ribs and lift me up, up above the throng, aiming me in the direction of the Hotel Cortez across the street. I'm blinded by the glare of the sun's reflection in the windows, rectangles of glass flashing in my eyes. Then, for just a second, through the bursts of white sunlight and a thousand hands raised in some kind of jubilation, I see a man's epic smile under a head of blazing red hair, all teeth and red-orange hair and his hand running through it before it waves at the crowd, waves distinctly at me, too, this man with fire in his hair and eyes of Olympian blue and a smile that envelops everyone appears for just a glimpse before I lose him again in the shimmer, but I'm above the tumult now, tears glistening on my flushed cheeks, pale and hot, numb and blind, bounced along to the chants of *¡Viva Kennedy! ¡Viva Kennedy! ¡Viva Kennedy!*

RED

HALF THE WORLD AS WE see it and half the world in red. That's how my little *carnalito*, the youngest of us, must see it. He's only five and already wearing horn-rimmed glasses, but now there is a lens of deep crimson laid over the right eye. It's meant to correct his "lazy eye," which is ironically the uncovered one. The effect of it makes him seem detached, his little face passive and stoic as an old man's. He's going to a different school, one he has to board a bus for, and the nature of that is a mystery to us. Why? Is something wrong with him? Does his indolent eye have something to do with it?

They call him pirate, the kids on the block. Red-eye they call him. *¡Ojo rojo!* They think up other comical epithets for him. They yell them from across the street. They say them to his face. He just maneuvers around the name-calling with his good eye, the red one, choosing to see what he wants in blazing red, thereby scorching to cinders all the cleverness and cruelty. My dad named him after a famous Mexican god; not a Toltec, though, but a singing idol of thc fifties and sixties with a voice like brown honey who died too young after gall bladder surgery. His last words were *No hay remedio*. It's no use. Something in my brother's demeanor agrees with that.

I see him standing on the corner for the bus. The little scab on his elbow. The part in his hair perfect all the way up to his crown. And I imagine how earth is pictured in one eye but in the other purgatory. Half the amber of the school bus, half the bright purple petals of the hydrangeas in our yard, half the desert blue of the Franklin Mountains, half the delicate orange blooms of the milkweed growing through the cracks in the gray sidewalk and half the single puff of dandelion skittering over the junipers, half the speckled blue-green of the collared lizard tasting the heat with its little pink tongue, half the faded-denim sky cottoned with clouds and half the walls of our house painted that drab ugly yellow, half the summer brown of my face; and half of all visible life enflamed in a harsh, implacable, all-consuming red. Even half his own red plaid shirt is redder through his blooded eye. He's standing in his own constant sunset. He's been imparted some vision of the last fiery days of men. Or half a vision, anyway.

His eye will mend. His detachment will resolve itself. And he will rejoin us in our schools. But the blood-red fires in the one lens of my *carnalito* burn into my own lazy eye the tenuous beauties of this world and the fears I harbor for them.

No hay remedio.

BLOOD AND COKE

ORDINARY DAYS AT THE BIG 8 Grocery Store. Mom is picking up tortillas and some Folgers and soda. She's in her pedal pushers with a bagful of Coke empties to redeem for some new ones. She's trying to herd all four of us by herself, but it's made more difficult by the distractions around. There's a row of cereal boxes with Tony the Tiger and shelves at kid eye-level crammed with cookies and candies and *piñatas* hanging from the ceiling in colors that don't even exist in our TV yet. I hear the clanging of shopping carts slamming into each other and cash registers ringing like someone just won a jackpot. My sister is trying to help my mom by holding my littlest brother by his belt-loop. I remember her forefinger through his pants' belt-loop. Then we're in line, some lady scowling at us for making all this *mitote*. The man at the register wears a white shirt and an apron with Big 8 emblazoned on the bib. His face is friendlier, kinder, and what hair he has left is slicked back with pomade. My mom is passing the Coke empties to the bag boy while she's counting out some change to pay. That's when the world cracks open and shows us what it's like inside.

I hear the explosive shattering of glass and my mother crying *AY!* All over the floor Coke bottles have broken, they've fallen over and broken and my mom has slipped in the syrupy soda. Just below the knee of her pedal pushers, I see the burbling of blood from one of her varicose veins choking out like water does when you first turn on the garden hose. My brothers are scared, they're crying, and my sister is trying to be brave but the look in her eyes betrays her concern. I'm

26

just staring like a fool at all this teeming blood mixing with the Coca Cola on the tiles, rushing all the way to my shoes. I can't tell if that's blood or soda spurting out of her leg.

The checkout man knows he should help but he sounds shrill and panicky and that makes my brothers scream even louder. He and the bag boy lift my mom off the floor and place her on the counter, which to me is kinda funny because there are bananas on the counter next to her. Someone's bananas. My mom does her best to sound reassuring, but it doesn't do any good. All this blood on my mother, all of it being mopped in buckets and still there's more. I can't hear her voice, only the low hum of her carbonated blood.

An ambulance comes with its sirens blasting and they put Mom on a gurney and now she's embarrassed at the attention. They wheel her out and load her into the white ambulance and she says, *Los veo en la casa*, but we don't believe her. For all we know, we'll never see her again. The ambulance pulls out and drives her away. Our mom is gone. But Mrs. Beltrán who lives nearby tells us she'll be home by tonight. She serves us *empanadas* and milk at her house and tells us it wasn't that bad a cut anyway. Just a few stitches and she'll be fine. The whole rest of the day we're trying to imagine what our lives will be like without her. I'm trying to picture my dad with another lady, and it doesn't work. I see nobody standing next to him except a guy wringing that black mop into a bucket.

My mom came back, like she said she would. But the Big 8 is gone now. The man at the checkout counter is gone. The piñatas, too. Even the tiny scar on my mother's leg is practically gone. But the memory of all the blood and Coke pulsing out of her leg, and my holy fear, it still astonishes me in my sleep from time to time.

CONSUELO

HER NAME IS CONSUELO AND she is our maid, our *criada*. She has something in her hands. A precious object. She comes down from the mountains of Mexico and takes a long bus ride to Ciudad Juárez, then walking over the Santa Fe Bridge to El Paso, boards another bus that takes her along the curve of the Lower Valley to our house. She lives with us, this lady whom everyone thinks is our *abuela*, because like our *abuela*, she commands our respect and rouses our love. Setting up her meager belongings in a small room near the kitchen, her comb, her picture of San Martín giving a piece of his cloak to a mendicant, her rosary and her small, crumbling Bible, beside the single bed that used to be my little brother's, she puts on her simple country dress and her apron with homemade rickrack. She's small and stout, with strong bowed legs that carry her through the house she spends all day cleaning. Her face dark and furrowed, her hair silver and tightly braided into a plait that hangs down her back like a staff, her hands rough and calloused as a man's, she cooks all our meals and calls for us when the plates are served. Wherever we are, we hear her summons and head for home. The food is so good that Kino and Marcos and the other kids want a plate too. She feeds us, feeds the dog, feeds the canaries in their cage, then feeds herself. All we know is her name, which is Consolation, which is perfect, since that is what she brings to my parents, who bust their asses day and night to make ends meet, which they never do, these ends that barely even pass each other across the room. She grows *hierbas* in the backyard and makes healing soups and teas for us when we're sick. Sometimes, when she's alone, when a lull in her daily labors permits, she sits and watches the *Canal Dos* on TV, the Spanish language shows. At night, after we've all had our dinners and are getting ready for bed, she goes to her room with the door closed, sits on her bed with her opened Bible and prays. There are times when she goes to see her family, she says she'll be gone two weeks, but two weeks can turn into four and then into eight because of difficulties at home or crossing-over issues. But six years of Consuelo, six years of her quiet folk singing as she hangs our clothes on the line, her sweeping the porch with that old broom, her stern admonishments to us for disrespecting our parents, six years of her practically raising us, invokes the deep *mestizaje* that lives in our blood, that reminds us we come from something older, simpler, and richer than the privileges we think are owed to us in this land.

This is a *retablo* of Consuelo, sitting on her bed with the door ajar just enough for a nine-year-old to peer through, this old woman with her hair unbraided, loose all the way down to her lap, with a sacred object in the cradle of her hands, what can it be but the apple we threw away, which she retrieved saying, Waste nothing of God's, and took to her room, and here it is, this sunken moldy apple, and Consuelo gingerly taking bites of it in the luminous mystery of faith.

KEENING

I'M ASLEEP IN MY ROOM when I hear crying. Like a baby crying. I open my eyes without moving a muscle to see if I can still hear it. Aside from the bitter, bracing wind outside, it's dead silent. I close my eyes, hoping I've dispelled whatever ambiguous sorrow happened to seize my sleep. Then I hear it again. Crying so thin and high and distant, it's almost air. And it's not from a baby. I sit up and listen. Yes, it's definitely coming from this house. I shift my legs out of bed as quietly as I can and open the door to my room. From down the hall, I can see the kitchen light on. The crying is more distinct now. A long thin keening that comes in through the teeth, I feel it in my teeth, that reedy cry threading its way along the thinnest part of the night and settling in my teeth, where it starts to reel me in like a doomed fish. Before I know it, I'm standing in my pajamas in the kitchen. Mom is making coffee. No, she's stirring soup in a stewpot. Steaming hot. Sitting down behind her, that's not my dad, but some man in an old straw cowboy hat with a fraying brim and dirty hatband. An older, darker man. Tufts of grey in his mustache. He's sitting at our kitchen table leaning close into another person, a younger woman, bundled up in blankets and *serapes*. Shivering violently. This is where the crying is coming from. That faint, almost whispered wail. The man is consoling her with hoarse words I can't make out. My mom says, What are you doing up? Go to bed. Go to bed now. Who are they, I ask. Nobody, she says. Go to bed, she says. I look down at the woman's feet and they are bare and dirty and raw and red and shivering like mad too. I see her face and my immediate impression is that she is ugly, her braided black hair framing an ugly face all red and covered in frozen snot. Her fingers all swollen and red too. They're both shaking with cold and maybe fear and maybe something else, some sickness they contracted just by being in our house. The man is saying, *Cálmate. Ya mero llegamos.* Which means they're leaving soon. My mom reaches into the stewpot with a pair of tongs and takes small towels out, and then wringing them over the sink, sets them on the table where the man places them on the woman's hands and feet. There's a bundle of wet clothes tied with baling wire by the back door. Also, a pair of boots, soggy tennies, and some balled-up socks. I feel my sister come in behind me, then my brother. My mother turns to us and explains that they are nice people and that they just need a little help. What kind of help, I ask. The back door opens and my dad comes in with snow flurries on his shoulders and his cap. He's been warming up the sedan outside. His face is clenched with worry as he looks down on the huddled pair. He asks the older man something and the older man gives him a small folded-up piece of paper. The woman is still crying and shaking her head like she's counting down a whole life's worth of mistakes. Mom says to me, Pour them some coffee, and I get the old percolator and two cups. My hand is shaking as I pour. I put the cups on the table and the woman turns her ugly face to me and whispers in the same keening tone, *Gracias.* While they drink their coffee, my dad tells the man in Spanish that they picked a bad night to cross. Every night is bad, he replies. Dad looks at the paper one more time and says, We should go. They put their socks and shoes on and they try to return the blankets to my mom, but she won't take them. Again, the woman says *gracias.* She stands, and I see then that she is pregnant. They pull the blankets up to their faces and start for the door. They follow my dad outside into the freezing snow. I can hear the loud motor of the car readying itself for some mission, then hear it shifting into reverse. My mom closes the door, latches it and says, *Ya. Se acabó.* Go to bed. We all go to bed shivering with some of their cold and some of their fear, and I fall asleep almost instantly and dream of a clay-colored woman with a figurine baby keening in the night.

MY FRIEND MEMÍN

THERE'S THIS CRAZY BLACK KID I know. He's always pulling shit, trying to do the right thing, but running up against scary people and dangerous situations. Getting in and out of trouble trying to help out his friends and maybe defending some principle for good measure. He usually ends up in his mama's arms or across her lap getting his bare ass spanked with a flat stick. But he's all right. He's my friend. His name is Memín Pingüín and he lives in the pages of his own Mexican comic book.

In the comics of our youth, all the people are white and their exploits are super-hero exploits with villains we've never seen in real life. But in the vividly colored pages of the comic books we find in Juárez, it's all Mexicans, and their cartoon balloons are filled with Spanish, from the cops and the teachers to the parents and street thugs. Memín is different, though. He's smaller than all the other kids in his striped teeshirt and cap with the brim pushed way high, but it's his dark skin, big ears and oversize lips that set him apart. A nasty stereotype, but I don't know that yet. He's my hero, and his adventures are real-world adventures that reflect the poverty, injustice and violence of everyday life in Juárez. I can't read Spanish, but I know Memín is a street survivor with a pure heart. Even when he suffers through calamities over which he has no control, he knows the difference between good and bad, kindness and cruelty.

That's before I have to fight him. 'Cause somewhere in school, sometime between third period and lunch, somebody heard Mike throw my name around like dirt and somebody else told him that I wanted to know what his deal was. And that's *pura mierda*, 'cause Mike and me are supposed to be best friends. But now *los chamacos* are saying I called him nigger and he called me wetback and so the word goes out that we're gonna settle this after school in the Big 8 parking lot. Neither of us can figure out how this started, neither of us knows how to get off the ride, the current's fierce and we need to save our strength for what's coming. All day I'm nervous, all day I'm thinking how can I get the nurse to send me home, all day I'm thinking he's going to beat me silly, all day I can hear Mike and me calling each other names we didn't know existed before this.

The bell rings like it's round one and we're rushed out of our classrooms straight down the halls and through the schoolyard, out of the gate and across the street to the parking lot. Everyone seems to know exactly what's going to happen but Mike and me. There he is across the tide of frenzied faces looking just like I feel, unsure, helpless, scared shitless. He's sweating all over, looking at me through bloodshot eyes like I did him some wrong, and I want to say, No, *vato*, we're *camaradas*, but behind me, hands are shoving me into him, shrill ten-year old voices yelling there he is, don't let him get away, beat that nigger, show that monkey who you are, while on his side, it's all get that spic, cut that dumb Frito Bandito face wide open. I clench my teeth just as the bell for round two goes off in our heads and before we know it we're flailing at each other with little fists, each blow calling out more ugliness, each kick taking us to that stark place where hurt is the rule, wrapped in each other's half nelsons, rolling in the hard gravel of the open lot with everyone shouting and laughing and raging 'cause it's 1968 and it's how we get along now, heat and hatred shaking the blood out of our noses, painting dumb hurt all over our faces while our ears ring with the crack of bonds broken and all of a sudden, it's done, we're pulled apart by a teacher and everyone disperses into their separate worlds but me and Mike held apart by our scruffs like cartoons panting and swinging at the air and the teacher shaking his head and yelling at us to go home and we do.

I don't talk to Mike after that. He don't talk to me. And Memín, I don't read his comic books anymore 'cause I figured out that shit is racist.

EL JUDÍO

I DON'T EVEN KNOW WHAT *Judío* means.

I thought it was his name. *El Judío*, my dad would say to my mom. *Ay viene el Judío.* Here comes the Jew. But what is a Jew? I never saw one before. I never heard that word before except in reference to Christ, King of the Jews. I thought it meant he was like Jesus. Three of my friends are named Jesús, and they aren't as half as good as the one in the Bible by a long shot. In fact, one of them shoots birds out of the mimosa trees with his BB gun for the pleasure of it and that seems completely the opposite of Jesus. But something about the way my parents say the words—*el Judío*—makes him seem special and sanctified, a man with the kind of spiritual dimension that demands his name be uttered in hushed tones. The Jew is coming today. Have you got enough for the Jew? *El Judío* is at the door.

One morning, I'm watching cartoons on the TV and the picture is flipping like crazy and the vertical hold doesn't work and my bladder is telling me to march in place before I pee myself in my pajamas. I hear a knock on the door and I open it. Standing real close to the screen door is a tall ruddy-faced man wearing a golf shirt with some design on the pocket, and at the base of his corpulent neck is a gold chain with a little star on it. He runs his hand through his short reddish hair and good-humoredly asks *¿Está Papá?*

My mom and dad are in the bedroom reading the paper while my brothers and my sister fight over the comics. All of them sprawled on the same bed in what is our Sunday morning ritual. But out here it's me and the man's benevolent smile. I like his watch, gleaming like a holy relic. I like his blue eyes squinting against the sun to peer into the dark of our house. I tell him to wait and I turn around and shout over the TV, MOM! DAD! *¡EL JUDÍO!* He blinks and blanches a little, never letting the smile teeter off his face, and then I see my mom come rushing out to grab me by the wrist and pull me into the kitchen with a mortified look. Then my dad yanking his pants on and counting out some cash takes my place at the door. A few words and a couple of bills are exchanged, my dad ending the whole thing with an earnest and apologetic *gracias*. Both of them incapable of letting their eyes meet.

Don't ever call him that, they tell me. That's not his name. His name is *Señor* Rubinsky. You got that? *¡Malcreado!* But that's what *you* call him, I protest. I hear you calling him the Jew all the time. That's none of your business, they fire back. He's *Señor* Rubinsky to you. David Rubinsky. *¿Entiendes?*

It turns out that David Rubinsky has loaned my dad some money to get him through our tough times. He's borrowed money from him for Christmas too, so we can get the bikes we plead and pray for. In fact, *Señor* Rubinsky has given countless low-interest loans to the many struggling Mexicans in the greasy spoon business and beyond. The local banks don't trust our dads much during these recession days. Why should they when these so-called unaccountables might just default and disappear over the border? The loans of *El Judío* are the difference between making the house payment or not, buying groceries or not, getting new clothes for school or not. Whatever they say behind his back, their gratitude for his service is deep and authentic. He's well regarded among these families. When he dies, they will come to his funeral, their cars lined up for miles to pay their respects to him. It's ironic that all my varied and valued experiences with Jewish people began with the most pernicious stereotype, but we were stereotypes then too. Poor backwater Mexicans who had to borrow against their own futures to realize them.

The following week, he's at the door again. This time he's wearing a paisley tie over a damp white shirt. I meet him at the door and politely say, Mr. Rubinsky. His ruddy complexion turns redder still and he looks at me like he's stung more by this salutation than by what I said the week prior, but then he pulls up his chin and confers on me the thinnest drollest smile.

Tell your *Papá* that *el Judío* is at the door.

EL MAR

APÁ THINKS WE NEED TO know the world so he gets us a globe. It's a Rand-McNally globe in a box with a stand and when it comes out, it's as big as a basketball. In fact, my little brother wants to bounce it on the floor. But once we put it on its stand and set it in rotation with a swish of our fingers, we know we're looking at our planet.

The first thing we do is find our home. We run our calloused little fingers across the brightly colored countries till we locate the United States and then pinpoint Texas. El Paso's not there, though. It's not even a dot. Only the major cities like Houston and Dallas get dots, and Washington D.C. gets a red star. Later on, one of us will scratch a crude X into the desert where our city should be just to confirm that we're actually there. Still, I'm proud beyond words to know that in our dusty little house we have a globe just like the one in our first grade classroom at Hacienda Heights Elementary.

They're not teaching us English there—it's just happening by default—but I'm keen to learn it fast. Maybe I just want to know what the teachers are saying to each other. Maybe I want to talk like the people on TV. I'm developing a vocabulary, too, though I don't know what that word means yet, and I'm extra dogmatic about my pronunciation. I learn that there's both a hard c sound and a soft c sound and I memorize the words that use them. Cowboy is one of the first words I learn, even before the word cow. I am in Texas, after all.

At home, I practice my pronunciation by picking the names of countries and places on our globe. I spin it fast and then stop it at random locations with my finger pressed over some exotic part of the world. Uganda, I say. Spin. Stop. South Korea, I say. Spin. Stop. Iceland. Some place names are easier than others. Spin. Stop. My finger's held hard against the middle of this blue expanse that I only know as *el mar*. I lift it and see a word I've never encountered before. OhKee-An. Ohkeean. What is the Pacific Ohkeean? It's spelled o-c-e-a-n but my tongue doesn't know how to deal with it. I've heard Pacific before, it's almost the name of the beer my *apá* likes to drink on his days off. I remember the label with the anchor and the mountains in the background framing the simple blue sea. Pacific has both the soft "c" and hard "c" sound. But how do I pronounce this other word except as Ohkeean? That must be it. I've never seen a body of water larger than the Rio Grande and it's mostly dammed to a trickle now but saying that word brings the vast open sea all the way here. In fact, this dry scrabbly desert we live in is an old prehistoric seabed itself. The surf, the spray of the crashing waves, the gulls scolding the surging swells. It's all in this curious ancestral word. Ohkeean.

The next day at school, I am looking for ways to demonstrate my knowledge. To show the teacher how well my pronunciation is coming along. I can't think of ways to bring it up. She's a nice, older black lady who seems to understand that the education we're getting is also teaching us to use a new language, and she's reading to us from some book, but I am hardly listening. I'm staring at the globe by the window, larger than ours, with defined topography, rivers, mountains and ohkeeans etched in and labeled. The sun through the louvered window is warming China and the Soviet Union. The world of knowledge. When she is done, the teacher orders us to take out our pencils and paper for a test on what she's read. I see my opportunity. I rush to the pencil sharpener and add a new tip to my stub. On the way back to my seat, I stop by the window and lay a dreamy hand on the smooth curve of the globe. Everyone is looking. The teacher too. She asks me, what are you doing.

I say, Nothing, miss. Just looking at the ohkeean.

She looks a little confused. Gently, she says, The what? The Pacific Ohkeean, miss. It's so big. I think I want to see it someday.

Then she gets it. I see her face beam with what seems like satisfaction and pride. She's even chuckling a little bit. Someone in the back of the room has started to snicker along.

Oh. I see. You mean ocean. It's pronounced o-shin. The Pacific Ocean.

Now the room is all laughter. Laughter drowning out the sounds of the surf, the seabirds, the swells and ripples on the beach. Laughter reaching into my mouth and ripping out my tongue for thinking it could own this new language so easily. I'm tensed up and loose around the knees at the same time, my face all on fire, and I blunder to my seat in abject shame. The teacher's calling for silence in the class, while I hear voices around me mutter *baboso*, *estúpido*, and other words for fool that I can't remember as well. The rest of the day drags on, the minute hand on the clock weighed down by all the mortification in my bones. In my head on the way out of school I keep hearing one word. One word.

I come home twenty years later. That old metal globe is still there in the closet, dented and rusty, crudely marked up with crayon. It's been bounced around like a ball, after all. I've traveled to many of the dots and some of the stars. I've lived much of my life near the sound of foghorns and seagulls and surf. I turn the globe in my hand to the word. It's still there. Still spelled the same way. Still insisting that to get the pronunciation right in the end, I had to get it wrong in the beginning. This was my entry into the complexities of our spoken English. But somewhere in the imagination of a little boy who has only beheld the sea on a beer bottle, there really is a special body of water known to him as an ohkeean.

THIEVES LIKE US

NEVER, NEVER CAN I TELL my mom. The mortification would kill her. And my dad, he'd be disappointed enough to find the belt and let me have it. So I keep it to myself, this unsaid potent thing, like an ingrown prayer. Only the grocer at the little market by Hacienda Heights Elementary and I know the truth. And the truth is he caught me.

We're standing outside the *tiendita* after lunch, me and two other seven-year-old *mocosos*. We got this crazy notion that it would be so cool to take some candy without paying for it. The old man behind the counter is slow and easily distracted, and lately he's seemed addled by all the Spanish the kids have been throwing around his store. Nervous and new at this, our little hearts rattling as hard as our teeth, we try talking ourselves out of it. We don't need the candy, I say, I got enough to buy some for all of us. It's not about the candy, the others say. Then what's it about? *Chingao*, we know what it's about.

Resolved at last, we put our plan in action. One kid walks in and starts to browse like he's got bucks to burn, while the other kid and I slink down the aisle where the candy is. Rows and rows of colorfully wrapped taffies, kisses and mints. The old grocer in his blue smock and rumpled black necktie is reading his paper. But the whole time, *ese*, he's reading us. The browsing kid goes over to ask him *Cuánto cuesta un bag de chips* while we shove as many hard candies into our pockets as we can and then casually turn around and make toward the free light of day. They're wedging themselves through the heavy glass door, and I'm almost there too, but before I can push it open, I feel the old man's claw squeezing my collarbone as he pushes me against the counter. He deftly locks the door with his other hand, stoops down to glare in my face and says, Empty your pockets. I'm in shock, I can't move, can't say a word, so he says it again, Empty your damn pockets, boy. I turn them out and three individually wrapped jawbreakers fall to the floor. Three stupid candies. I can't believe that's all I managed to get.

He snatches them off the floor and slaps them on the counter, then clamping his hand hard against the base of my neck, directs me to a cramped storage room in the back where he plants me on a cardboard box and stands over me with his arms crossed. His panting is loud as a bull's. I'm sobbing, shivering with terror, my pants already warm with pee. Then he spits something like this right in my face:

You little thief. You people are all just little thieves. You thought you could pull one over on me, but I got you, didn't I? Didn't I? I should call the police, let them deal with you! You want that?

I'm wailing and shaking my head, blind with tears, smearing my wet nose across my dusty brown arm. The old guy's face is all fire and whiskers as he rages on: I'm keeping my eye on you. Stealing is your nature, it sticks to you like dirt. *Comprende*, boy? Then he shoves me out the door, leaves me standing in the open to cry myself home.

Two days later, I have my First Holy Communion.

A shimmering Sunday morning in my white short-sleeved shirt and clip-on tie. A procession into San Antonio Church with my catechism classmates. Parents standing inside at their assigned pews, faces beaming, Kodaks flashing. We kneel in place before the altar, rosaries draped meaningfully over our clasped hands. The Father in his perfect white vestment spreads his arms wide and begins the Mass. *En el nombre del Padre y del Hijo y del Espíritu Santo . . .*

Amen, we reply in unison.

We go through our prayers, the readings from the Old Testament and the Gospels, we conduct the call and response with the Father and stand, sit and kneel in due piety, just as we were taught. But under my ironed white shirt, every chamber in my heart is flooded with shame. I still feel that grocer's hand, the pain in my collarbone, I see the candies on the floor and walk the heavy walk home in my pants reeking of pee. The Father gives a short sermon on the magnanimous grace of Jesus, who even as he was nailed to a cross, forgave the sins of one of the thieves crucified with him. Jesus assured the penitent thief a place in heaven, the Father says, because he renounced his sinful ways. But when he glances in my direction, I see the grocer's face red and spiteful denying any such place for me.

Now, as we prepare to take the Eucharist and fuse the body of Christ with our own, we make our confessions. The priest enters the confessional and we line up to enumerate our sins before him. The disgrace sucks all the blood down to my feet and I feel faint. I feel sick. How can I tell him? How can I admit that I stole candies just for the fun of it? Father, I'm nothing but a little thief. I don't deserve absolution. I'm unredeemable shit.

Approaching the confessional, my mind drifts to that forgiven thief, whom I envision as Cantinflas, the funny man of those old Mexican movies at the drive-in. I think of him prowling around heaven in his rags, wondering at his good fortune. I see him marveling at the splendor and riches that Divinity has laid before him, the crowns of light, the piercing rays of heavenly grace, the pealing bells of holiness and joy. He's in the company of saints and angels and now all the *gente* he's known are washed clean of their sins too, stepping through what looks like a human carwash, coming out on the other side all blow-dried, waxed and shiny. I see him greeting them, embracing them warmly, with tenderness. Then I see him nimbly picking their pockets. I see him robbing seraphim too, filling his bag with unanswered prayers, breaking into heaven's vault to steal everyone's jawbreakers and running off with the loot like the bandit he is. Because it's his nature. Always a thief. Thief everlasting. Even at this sacred moment, while I kneel before the waiting ear of the Father, he's creeping in through the unlatched window of my soul to steal the self-incriminating words from my mouth, 'cause five minutes later, I'm stepping out of the confessional without having said them and lining up to receive the host on my absolvéd tongue like it's candy. Into the cleansing glare of the noonday sun I come, newly made in Christ by His grace, and the dirty grace of a sanctified thief, strutting down the gilded streets of paradise in his peed-on pants.

MY MONSTERS

I LOVE MY MONSTERS. I watch them all the time. They roar and rampage and scare the hell out of everyone. But not me. I'm old enough to know they exist only in scary movies. Still, I love them so much, I troop to the tiny 16 Food Corral convenience store at the butt end of every month to ferret through the magazine racks for them. Usually, they're stacked at the back of the lower shelf and all I have to do is reach past *True Crime*, *Mad Magazine*, and *Guns and Ammo*, and there they are: the Wolfman, Frankenstein, the Mummy, Dracula, the Beast from Another Planet. All in the pages of *Famous Monsters of Filmland*. I flip through and there's Bela and Boris, Lon and Lon Jr., Cushing and Christopher Lee, movie stills from the great Universal Studios horror flicks and low-budget sci-fi of the '50s, interviews with directors, makeup artists, stop-motion animators. Everything a brown kid with a runaway imagination needs to know about movie horror is in here.

My room is a shrine to scary movies. Painted models of the Phantom of the Opera and the Mummy glower from my dresser, and Frankenstein and the Alien from This Island Earth glower from the posters on my walls. I have pencil drawings of otherworldly creatures everywhere, inspired by the boxloads of magazines I keep under the bed. Yes, there really *are* monsters under my bed. Everyone wonders how they have this hold on me. Don't you think it's a little immature? Don't you think it's kinda retarded? they ask. But I don't understand the questions. All I know is that on the days when it's hard to be me, these monsters are my solace. I put on fangs and practice snarling like a vampire in the mirror. I walk around sullenly scratching my palms on full moons because this is the first sign of a deadly metamorphosis. Open up the family dictionary and look up lycanthropy. Next to the definition, someone with my twelve-year-old cursive has scrawled "Oh god, it's true!" I keep the severed, decomposing head of Dorian Gray in my closet, a Styrofoam wig-head that I carved a mouth and eye holes into, covered with clay, and painted. It almost looks like the one in the magazine.

This day the sun is plummeting faster than I expect as I walk down this little street called Manor Place to see if my monsters have come. I pass a house with wainscoting over these little red bricks that make it look prim and toy-like. There's a kid sitting on the porch, a little younger than me and fatter, and he's got a look on his face that says Don't look at me, but I do. His face is puffy with some kind of anger. He's got a plastic Tyrannosaurus Rex and he's forcing its open jaws onto the long neck of a Diplodocus. He's doing it with personal fury. There are noises in the house that sound like laughter, but it's a woman crying. A man yelling and throwing things and a woman crying. The kid doesn't look up and now I know he's not puffy from anger. I head on to the store.

When I get there, I almost forget why I'm there. I buy a Creamsicle and half-heartedly turn to the rack. The old guy says, It hasn't come in yet. Try again tomorrow, he says. I nod and head back down Manor Place. Now it's so dark, it should be night, but the last traces of day linger in the high clouds. I can hardly see my hand in front of me, while high overhead a long ghostly thread spools from a jet plane. I pass the house again, and this time the porch light is on and it's quiet as death. The kid is gone but his dinosaurs are there. I walk up the sidewalk to the porch and look them over. The head of the Diplodocus is gnawed down to a nub. But not by the T Rex. I hear some noises in the house and move away across the lawn. There is a window, and I imagine it's his room. I imagine pinned all over his room these horror movie posters and on his desk, delicate pinprick brushes, small vials of glue and paint by the unfinished model of the Wolfman with that frozen snarl on his face. I imagine him in bed unable to sleep, chewing on the head of his dinosaur while he's thinking of ways to beat me to my magazine, which comes to the 16 Food Corral for me, and a hate rises in my throat for him. Then I imagine him reading my magazine with unwavering focus while the walls of his room thump violently over the yelling and crying of parents in their lycanthropic breaks, and I hate him all the more for that.

BEN

THEN THERE'S BEN. EVERY WEEK the old man comes by the house on his way to somewhere. He knows I'm waiting. Sometimes I'm outside and he sees me and waves from across the street, and the time it takes him to get to me lasts as long as a dream. He's in no hurry. The world inches along with him.

I know he has something for me. He always does.

Sometimes, it's little plastic cowboys with chaps flared and guns drawn. Coins with holes in the center from other countries with names I can't pronounce. Old Louis L'Amour paperback Westerns with the colorful cover illustrations. He even gives me his entire stamp collection. I see his spotted, crinkled foolscap hands, holding this book with stamps from all around the world, and through his wire-rimmed glasses, I see the scuffed grey of his eyes as he drawls, I'm too old to finish it, son. You'll have to do it for me.

My mom knows him from the soda fountain at the Gunning-Casteel Drug Store where she works. He comes and has his coffee and sandwich and chats with her. He sits like something out of another time, cross-legged in his baggy khakis with suspenders over a plain cotton shirt. On his head sits a well-worn wide-brimmed fedora that he never takes off. It's his soft ruddy leathery face that draws me in. The face of a man who's seen more good life than I think I ever will. A face that looks like the grandfather of my old black-and-white fantasy reel.

Finally, he's on my porch smiling and I say, Hi Ben. He nods and says something about the heat and the days counted since the last rain. He even has a little book where he keeps the tally on the dry spell, a remnant from his old rancher days. He asks me to put out my hand and I do. And on it he places a hard, red gourd-like thing. I've never seen anything like it before. It's a pomegranate, he says. He takes out his knife and pries it open and shows me the embedded seeds like drops of blood in a bowl of wax. I pick a few off the blade and they're the richest, sweetest nuggets my mouth has ever tasted. Beaming with all the teeth he has left, he says he has a small orchard in his yard full of them. September sun has been good to them. He says, Come by sometime, son, I'll give you more. Then he's off. Seems like ten minutes later, I can still see him down the street, shuffling like a patient tortoise on his way to lunch.

Where is Borneo? Where's Luxembourg? The stamps in the stamp book seem to come from made-up lands. Fantasy places where people like Ben can come and go at will and have adventures that they keep hidden under their fedoras. Does he ride his pony there and chase after bandits and reap his reward in otherworldly fruit? Are these stamps taken from the letters of a lady-love who wanders the world for him? I'm thinking all this one day later that month when three of my buddies show up on their bikes and beckon me. I ride off with them like the posse in my Louis L'Amour.

One of them says, I know. Let's go get some grenades. Grenades? What are you talking about, I ask. What grenades? They laugh and tell me to follow them to this place. We ride into an alleyway and park our bikes against the tumbleweeds and clamber over a wall into this lush open garden with grass so green it's almost blue. There's a clump of small trees, wide at the base, thick with pomegranates. *Granadas, ese*, my buddy says with a wink. We yank a bunch of the biggest ones off the low branches and shove them into our pockets and inside our shirts, some of them already bleeding their juice into our hands, and this is how we know we're stealing. Then I hear the slap of a screen door and we turn tail for the wall and leap over it giggling and snorting like idiots. I look over my shoulder and see this bald-headed old geezer, shirtless and pale, waving his hands, feebly shouting. Goldurn punks! Git! Git out, you! Go on! You're trespassin'! But we're already ripping down the alley on our bikes, dropping loose pomegranates in our wake.

Later, we're at the levee by the *río* digging our faces into the *granadas*, laughing at our escapade, going over it again and again, embellishing things here and there until it becomes the heroic exploit of our summer. Then I picture again that comical screaming old man in my head and I realize it's Ben. Ben of the old fedora and the slow walk and the little gifts. And these are Ben's pomegranates. I feel my face on the inside turning as red as the little seeds in my throat. I feel Borneo and the cowboys of Louis L'Amour slipping away. I feel a hole in my heart as wide as a coin, and then I throw up. The sickly, cloying taste of the pomegranates rises in my gullet and up they come. All my buddies shriek with laughter and add that one more crazy item to the exploits of the day.

I see Ben walking by again, but I won't go out to see him. I won't go and see what new thing he has for me today. He's looking from across the street, hoping to see me step out on the porch and wave, but I won't. I won't do it. He walks on. He wipes his wire-rimmed glasses against his old plaid shirt and walks on.

OUR OTHER HOUSE

THESE WEEKENDS WHEN WE ARE little *mocosos* come and go like dreams, but encased inside of them are fainter, stranger *sueños* that make so little sense, we brush them off like the airy cotton from the cottonwoods of our old house. They start with Mom home alone with us and us watching Johnny Quest or playing with our cap pistols while she hangs the wash on the line outside. My father's white work shirts puffing up like ghosts with the hot desert breeze. Suddenly, she gets a notion in the middle of the day and abruptly orders us to put on our shoes and herds us into the car. The Ford Galaxie is almost on empty, so there's always a stop at the pump station where she buys fifty cents' worth of regular. The whole way there, she won't tell us where we're going.

We're just driving around, she says.

But she always winds up in that strange little ward, driving real slow down the same pleasant cul-de-sac, looking out at one particular house with people washing their cars or mowing their lawns or some kids playing on the sidewalk, racing the sprinklers back and forth. We ask her, What are we doing here, Mom. She says that she wants to see the true lives of real people, see the real house we'll live in someday. This is her dream neighborhood, she says, but there's nothing wistful in her voice about it, and I can't see her eyes in the rear-view mirror, only her bangs draped over her brow like Natalie Wood in This Property Is Condemned. She leans forward in her seat to get a better view of the pretty bungalow with its well-tended lawn and ivy winding up the trellis on the porch, and we all lean forward too, but somehow we can't see what she sees.

In these car dreams, I think about how different I would be if I lived in that house. I wonder if I'd be happier, if I'd like myself more. One time I think I see my other self standing at the window looking back at me. Another skinny brown kid in a checkered shirt, only not so skinny and not so brown and the sun catching some of the hazel in his eyes. Catching some other thing as well, some question or resentment or guardedness about something forbidden. Eyes that say don't stop here.

Anyway, Mom drives by once, maybe twice, then turns to go home. We're strangely silent all the way back, each of us in our own secret haze. I'm teasing back the vinyl from the armrest with thumb and forefinger, laying bare the foam stuffing underneath as the AM radio sputters out some oldie from my mother's youth. It's her youth I think we're drifting on, the distillation of her own private hopes, now distant and residing in a cul-de-sac we'll see only from our Galaxie. That's *almost* us in the house there, with a greener lawn, a diorama of the family we could have been.

After a while, we stop going there. The weekends fill up with shopping sprees for school supplies and rides to my brothers' junior league football games and my trumpet lessons. Our Dad's Sundays open up, and when we're not spending them at home with Mom and him, we're picnicking in Ruidoso or driving to Carlsbad Caverns. In the years to come, though, I'll head out on my own to find that cul-de-sac. I'll cruise around countless times looking for that secret house. I won't find it; even to this day, I can't remember the street name. It's an ill-fitting memory of a place that never was. But if I close my eyes and follow the crumbs of some old longing playing on the radio, I can almost dream myself back to the idyll of our other house, and to him, reflected at the window.

SATURDAY

LISTEN TO THAT. THAT'S JUÁREZ you hear. That is where we are once a month on Saturdays. Riding along *la Avenida de las Américas* with that crazed accordion erupting from the radios all around. *Paleteros* taking their smoke break on the curb. There's the old cop who watches over our parked station wagon for a modest ten-dollar *mordida* from my dad. He's got a gold tooth in his smile and duct tape around the handle of his gun. His armpits wet and ripe with his morning smell but it's all a morning smell here. There's the *Centro Pronaf* where we do our shopping, my mom filling her cart with things half the cost of those at our Piggly Wiggly. Plus the tortillas are always better here, *chamacos*. A short walk through the *mercado*, where the old woman sits on a stool hawking the leather belts in her leather hands, and the *piñatas* dangle from the ceiling like papier-mâché gods, and piles and piles of *serapes* and blankets amid black velvet paintings of Jesus and Pancho Villa and the Beatles. And the *taquitos* are fresh here. Sit outside and eat some with a Fanta while Dad throws a few *centavos* on the street to delight the urchins with feet hard as stone, and that little one looks like someone he remembers, maybe himself as a boy, and he gives him a half-dollar coin more. Poverty is obvious in Juárez; it's out in the open, tugging on our sleeves, thronging around us for whatever surplus scraps of hope we've got. Now it's time to see the barbers. My younger brother and I, and my youngest brother too, we're all trying to cultivate styles that suit the time and we take pains to instruct the barbers how we want it cut, *un poquito* longer on the sides and the back, shorter on top, and can you make sideburns on us too like in those music shows on TV and the album covers of the bands we love, long hair is the way to go, *por favor*, and they nod like they understand, like they're on our side, slapping their barber capes over us, spinning our chairs around so we don't face the mirror, and then it's all a chaos of clippers and trimmers and shears, our chins pushed into our sternums so all we see is our tufts wafting to the floor in clumps. We're sobbing like fools when we finally see our scrawny bald heads in the *pinche* mirror, my father looking up from his *Memín Pingüín* comic book to find us wailing while those perfidious barbers sweep the frazzle-ends of our yearning into a fuzzy little mound for the trash bin. Dad pays them for their trouble and appeases us with some Mexican Coke, but it's scant comfort, we're so disgusted at how four-sided we look, plus that one with the pompadour left nicks on my neck and even nipped my ear, but Dad salutes us 'cause we look like Ft. Bliss soldiers, making us bawl even more; the world is over as far as we're concerned. That's when Mom takes over. While my dad tanks up the station wagon for five bucks, she takes us by the hands and guides us just a few steps down the buckling walkway past the bony dog dozing under his halo of flies through the open door of a warehouse so we can behold in its dark metal swelter this astounding vision: a young man thin and shirtless, spearing a long hollow pole into a kind of furnace and taking out a glowing mass of molten red-orange light, hissing against the cooling air, pieces of it spattering on the cement floor like lava. Then he performs this magic: he blows into the pole and the glob swells as he spins it over a flame, shapes it with another metal rod into something unimaginable, shapes it into glass, it's glass he's breathing, crafting it into forms that begin to take on color and character; it's a vase, then a panther, then a long lamp-like sculpture, wondrous and ghostly, this gleaming young Vulcan breathing structure into throbbing suns of incandescent glass. Now we're not thinking haircuts or sodas or feeling anything but the lulling heat of this primeval forge where the most elegant fragile fires are blown into being. All the way home, on the slow bumper-to-dented-bumper drive over the bridge back to El Paso, as we shove chili-powdered *chicharrones* into our mouths, we marvel at the genius of Saturday, *ay sábado, mi sábado,* you took our hair and paid us back with a glimpse at how this beautiful messy world blazed when it was first created, might blaze again someday.

THE MEXICAN I NEEDED

HERB ALPERT IS THE MOST beautiful Mexican I have ever seen. This is what I believe in 1960-something. My mom has a robust collection of albums by this man and when she plays them, the house seems to break into that sunny Tijuana Brass smile. We're not sure how she manages to afford so many of them. But there they are. The Lonely Bull. Going Places. Casino Royale. What Now My Love. And of course, that wet dream of every boy across the country, Whipped Cream and Other Delights. While the cheery horn plays through our hi-fi console, I'm all over that naked girl on the album cover. Sitting in a cake with cream covering all her strategic parts, she's eyeing me as she licks a dollop of the risings in my own body off her finger. And yet, in the end, it's Herb Alpert himself who intrigues me.

I know the songs are ridiculous, even at my age. Rock is maturing into a social movement all around us and grabbing all the cool in the world, which makes these jaunty tunes like "Mexican Shuffle," "Tijuana Taxi" and "Surfin' Señorita" seem as mild and middle-brow as his renditions of "Love Potion No. 9" and "Walk, Don't Run." After all, it's our parents' music. But something about that well-kempt man and his shiny trumpet draws me in. He's so easygoing and smooth, the hair on his forehead angled like a beret, his smile roguish and sly 'cause he's got that girl on his arm who can't take her eyes off him. Mom says, *Este hombre es guapísimo*, fanning herself with her open hand to prove it. But I need no corroboration.

I study his songs, the corny ones like "Spanish Flea" and

the more sentimental numbers like "Marching Thru Madrid," trying to decode in the music that special quality that makes him so damn suave. One song in particular feels more Mexican than anything on the Juárez radio stations my dad prefers. For me, "The Green Leaves of Summer" bares the essential soul of that ancient *país* across the *río*. Those percussive pulses of Mexico, it's gotta be the real deal, right? It has to be, if it's stirring up the Mexican in me.

I play the albums end to end until I can see myself playing his golden horn. But to be him I gotta have a trumpet. Where am I gonna get one? How in this crummy corner of El Paso is a ten-year-old brown dreamer gonna find a shiny trumpet like the one in Herb Alpert's hands? I beg Mom to get me one, but she just laughs. Maybe when you're older. I need it *now*, though, I want to be cool now.

So I make my own. On a shoebox lid, I draw the outline of a trumpet. I cut it out, meticulously shaping the valves, the curve of the bell and the intricate mouthpiece. I color it in yellow crayon, which is as close to gold as I get. When it's done, it doesn't seem like much. It looks smaller than the one on the album covers and none of the pistons move, but it fits in my hands, which is all that counts. Just add music. When noone is home, I set the needle on "The Lonely Bull," and when it starts, I'm breathing notes into that trumpet with such ease, it's like the air for that music was always in me. Herb Alpert is in my lungs.

I play "Tangerine," "Blue Sunday," "Zorba the Greek," and "Struttin' With Maria" in the living room as I lead the band in one number after another. The mouthpiece gets moist and crumbly from my spit, but I don't care. I'm coasting on kid euphoria, acting out a fantasy that carries me out of this grey little house in the desert to zones that throb in the grooves of those records. My own 33 rpm rabbit hole that nobody knows about.

Until they do. My kid brothers find my shoebox trumpet

stashed under the bed. Except that instead of being disgusted, they're actually intrigued. *Carnal mayor* has a new bag and it looks kinda fun. Later, when we're older and our hair is longer, when we discard our baby dreams for dreams of rock and roll, we fashion guitars out of cardboard boxes and drum kits out of empty ice cream canisters from the soda fountain where Mom works to jam along with CCR, the Grassroots, Steppenwolf and Santana.

That's the thing about our home. Fantasy was indulged. I wouldn't have dreamed if it hadn't been. My dad tolerated music in our house and Mom encouraged it, and more than once, I caught them smiling in on my performance to "Spanish Flea," even if it came out of a fake cardboard trumpet with a crayoned-on mouthpiece. Not one of us ever learned music. Not one of us ever played an instrument. Like it mattered. One day, thirty years later, someone tells me Herb Alpert is actually of Ukrainian and Romanian extraction. But what do I care? To me, he'll always be the Mexican I needed for dreaming.

LA MIGRA

THAT'S WHAT WE CALL THEM. That's how I have always known them. *La migra* is a derogatory term, but we don't even think of it like that. It's just what they are. Ever since we moved into the Lower Valley, the green and white cruisers of the Border Patrol have been everyday fixtures in our lives.

In the early days, they are older guys who take their jobs in stride. They ride on patrol like hired cowboys roping in the errant dogies. Or maybe more like Texas Rangers patrolling the wild frontier. They know a large portion of the migrants will slip through their net, and they know many of those they catch will be back through the fence in a matter of days. They're philosophical about their mission. What's the harm in a few *mojados* coming through? Don't we need the manpower anyway?

Then in the late '60s and early '70s, there's a new breed of officer. Stern all-American types, ex-soldiers who got their asses kicked in the jungles of Vietnam and now look to settle that score with these wetbacks and their smuggled maryjane. They take the job seriously, consider themselves a cut above the average city cop. What they do is harder and makes a bigger difference in the complicated world of *la frontera*. That's my take on them, anyway.

I start noticing something else in the early '70s, though. Maybe it was always there and I just didn't see it, or maybe it's a result of the recession and the lack of good-paying jobs. Suddenly there are more *Chicanos* manning the vans and cruisers. The iron in the faces, the edge in the eyes, it's all the same, only now the faces and eyes are brown. The badges say Marquez, Armendariz, Lujan. Some are even rougher than their Anglo counterparts. It doesn't matter that their parents probably came over the same river with the same intention; one generation is all it takes to keep the past and the legacy of their migration at bay. They're American now and this is how they show it.

We're used to them, how they slow down whenever we're outside drinking Cokes by our bikes. The officer in his Aviator sunglasses looks us over, scouring our skinny bodies for the one thing that marks us as foreign. Kino and I point to each other and mouth the words: take him, take him. My sister takes exception, though. She thinks the border cop is checking her out, and she's probably right. But the fact that he's even scrutinizing us this closely is disturbing. His look lingers just long enough to make us feel like strangers to ourselves. All the *mojaditos* that we generally scowl at when we spy them tramping restlessly past our house; he's consciously connecting them to us. We're nothing like them, we've conditioned ourselves to say. We're legal, born on this side. But the border cop with his steady gaze is telling us with his look that the distinction is very thin. Thin as the lenses on his Aviators. Thin as a line on a map.

This day I am waiting for the bus to take me downtown to see a movie. The bus stop is just across the street from my house. The Border Patrol comes up the street and stops right at the curb. It's that Mexican officer again and he's wearing the same reflective shades. His partner is this white guy who looks like he's been badly sunburned. Both of them are giving me a once-over that makes me nervous. It's the Mexican who talks to me.

You seen anyone go by here lately?

No.

Anyone wearing a red tee?

No.

You're wearing a red tee.

I look down at myself and look at the red tee-shirt with the lettering of some band I used to think was bitchen.

Where you from, kid, he asks.

Here.

Where.

America.

Where do you live?

Right there. I point at my house.

What's the address?

I recite it for him like my life depends on it.

Then he does something unexpected. He removes his shades and asks me, *¿Hablas español?*

Now I'm trapped. I want to say no, even if it's a lie. 'Cause to admit that I speak Spanish would put me in the other guy's red tee. Just like that, he's made me ashamed of my original tongue, forced me to deny my father's language and thereby deny my father and his fathers before him. And the crazy thing about it is this man is using that very same Spanish against me. There's only one thing I can say.

A little.

¿Quieres pasar tus días allí?

What?

You know what I said.

No sir.

He smirks at my lie and looks me right in the face. Do you want to spend your days over there?

I'm an American, sir.

Barely. Where you going?

The movies.

In my peripheral vision, I sense my mom at the front door and the white officer nudges his partner, who puts on his Aviators and tells me to keep an eye out for a *mojado* with a red tee-shirt. Which is what I see reflected in the lenses.

If you spot him, you call us, okay?

These guys are the butts of our jokes. Now they have me shaking all over. They say, Have a good day and drive on down the street. The bus comes right after they leave and I go to my James Bond double bill at the Palace Theatre downtown, and the whole time I'm watching the screen, I am hating these men and thanking them at the same time. Because they're right. I am the guy in the red tee. I am him. And he is me.

THE LITTLE WOODS

ALL THE BLISSFUL PLACES HARBOR danger. They bring you to heights you'll never experience anywhere else, but then they teach you other things, too. Things you'll learn later anyway, but the way you learn them here becomes a sickness you carry the rest of your life. This virus called knowledge.

We're riding there now. My brothers and me and Marcos and Kino. Watch us tearing through the streets of Cedar Grove on our bikes like runaways. Shirts billowing behind us like superhero capes. A man watering his lawn looks at us and wishes he was ten years old, too. If he only knew where we're going. But he wasn't there under the willow tree at Kino's house when Kino told us about this secret place he heard of. He called it "the little woods," and that was enough to captivate us, thrill us, charge us with the duty to seek it out. Our own summer Shangri-La.

We get to the end of the paved road where St. Paul's church sits like one of God's forgotten outposts and just beyond that, we see it. The little woods. We pull up right to the edge of it and look down at this dense little clump of stubby trees and scrub brush submerged in a wide irrigation channel. It doesn't seem like much from this vantage, but once we descend into the trails winding up and around all the trees and hills and sand pits, the woods seem to go on forever. *¡Chingao! ¡Puta verga!* It's perfect! It's our new private bike course where we can speed through the length of the woods and find air and fall in the bushes and skin our knees and laugh and scream and cuss like pirates and ride the high of our crazy blood till we drop! And after that we ride some more!

Sitting in one of the myriad sagebrush hollows that we find all over this scrappy desert eden, panting like crazy dogs, the sun painting the pits of our tee-shirts with sweat, we tell the happy lies that all boys tell each other when they feel their lives throbbing with possibility. Who's got the bigger dick. Who saw their sister in the shower. Who was chased by a gang and almost got beat up. Who has seen the strippers at the Martinique Club. We promise that next time, someone brings cigarettes. The sun is stretching shadows to remind us it's time to go home, but we're coming back for sure. Tomorrow for sure. We straddle our bikes, and then one of us, my littlest brother, I think, finds something weird thrown back under the tumbleweeds. It's a long white wad of cotton and there's charred blood on it. We think it's blood. Strange, *ese*. What could it mean? What happened here? There's a couple of empty Coors bottles too. Then we come upon this little elastic thing half-caked in dirt. I pick it up and show it to the others. What is this? It's a rubber, Marcos says. A what? What's that? What's it for? Marcos turns pale and all the rest of us follow suit as I fling the damned thing back into the bushes. We know what it's for.

Next day we coast into the little woods again, blasting through the afternoon like happy demons. We trash our bikes a couple times, but they're hardy and can stand up to it. We have a silent compact not to ride near that dirty little hollow and that makes it a great day.

Then some time later, at the summit of July, when the heat is so unbearable the sky itself is blanched and sere, everyone goes for a swim at the community pool. But I stay home. I'm writing stupid poems about stupid things that I think are deep but are really someone else's insights put through the sieve of my stupid mind. I want to ride out to the little woods by myself. To suck up the specialness of that grove all by myself. So I go.

I pedal over the shadow of the cross on the steeple of St. Paul's and roll down into the obstacle course that we've made of the little woods. I see more tire treads on the course, which means that other kids have found our secret place. Maybe it was their secret to begin with and we invaded it. For now, it's all mine. Riding and braking and soaring over the hills and bumping over logs and snaking through the bristling weeds and dusty leaves of scrub oak and manzanita, I feel the meter of my real poem pounding through the handlebars, all boyhood and body heat. Panting hard, I stop my bike to earn the moment in stillness.

That's when I see them. He's hunched over her, with his pants and underwear in a gnarl around his knees, his bare buttocks clenching and unclenching in rhythm. And her brown legs are splayed flat and motionless, like she's dead. Her hands are clamped onto the slender trunks of brush directly over her. Nothing under them but dirt. They are doing it in the dirt. He's making grunts and noises that sound like Spanish underwater. And she's repeating *ay, ay, ay, ay* . . . until she says, *Cuidado, pendejo* and slaps him hard on the shoulder. He laughs and adjusts his position and settles into her again with a groan. But she sees me without even looking in my direction and immediately throws him aside, covering her breasts as she stands directly in my path. I pedal down past her to get away, but she screams something that I can't make out and spits at me. The words miss but the spit lands right on my face. I ride all the way home and sit in my room until I realize I want to take a bath. My nakedness in the tub reminds me of them and I feel ugly. So dumb and ugly.

Over the rest of the summer and the summer to come, we go back to the little woods. We find more condoms and tampons amid the weeds and sometimes soiled underwear and sometimes needles and cotton balls. We see two guys sitting around a clump of beer cans smoking *mota*. They look at us with eyes full of dull hazard. We see a group of people, four or five, changing clothes silent as thieves and Kino says they must be *mojados* hiding from *la migra*. All this we can live with. What we can't bear are the other kids that are using our little woods for their own adventures. For one thing, they're better at maneuvering their bikes through the trails than we ever were. Then my mom hears that some girl was raped there one night and makes us swear never to go again. That's the end of the little woods for us.

When the junior high school is built, the property is just a stone's throw away from the little woods. I'm an eighth grader spending the lunch hour with my friends the Rodela twins playing chase through my old stomping ground, running and dodging and squealing with joy and for a while my childhood treasure is restored, but when one Rodela lobs a large rock at the other and smashes him badly in the face, cleaving wide his forehead with blood, we get in trouble and the principal commands us to stay on school grounds. One of you is gonna get himself killed out there, he drawls. For the rest of the year, I see the little woods through the chain link fence of the schoolyard.

I don't know when it happened. It must have been in my senior year, maybe later. Maybe it happened after I left for college. The little woods were burned, bulldozed over and covered with landfill. St. Paul's was renovated and its parking lot enlarged, the junior high school remodeled and added to, and the space where the little woods used to be is now an unremarkable stretch of barren real estate. There's nothing there to tell lies about. Nothing of ourselves and the hardscrabble world hidden in the weeds. Just a dried tract in the desert with an almost imperceptible depression, like a grave.

THE COTTON

I GO INTO THE COTTON. When the world is too much and I can't take the yelling in the house, I go into the cotton fields and ponder. There's one three-acre lot right over the wall in our backyard and another across the street on the right flank of our house, the last agricultural holdouts in our modest working-class subdivision by the river, and in a few years they won't be there at all. It'll be all ugly little houses like ours. But in this phase of my childhood, these fields are a real and steady comfort in my life, especially when the crop is tall and bristling with cotton blossoms.

We're playing hide-and-go-seek in the waning rose of dusk. My brother is counting backwards to one with his head bowed against the front door of our *chante*. Everyone scatters. Someone hides behind the juniper bush. Someone hides under the old rusty Opel with the weeds growing through the floorboards. Someone crawls into the big pipe in the drainage ditch with the crayfish. I go into the cotton. The stalks are four feet high, the green leaves as stout as the burgeoning bolls of white fiber. I run through the narrow ruts between the rows until I'm twenty feet in and kneel on the cold, caked earth feeling the pointy leaves against the back of my neck. I'm panting with the thrill of my hiding place, and to hear the countdown to "ready or not," I hold my breath for a second and listen. In that stillness, I begin to hear sharper, shallower panting coming from behind me. Slowly, I turn my head and see a girl crouched in the bower of the same rut. She's dark as an Indian, her black hair braided and pinned around her

68

head like a crown, and she's clutching close to her chest a mesh tote bag. Soaking wet in her blouse and cut-offs, her feet shod with muddy canvas sneakers, she keeps silent and immobile, like she's growing out of the ground with the cotton. Her eyes fix on mine and I realize I'm in her hiding place. But she's in mine too. We're cowering in the same lair, but for different reasons. I'm hiding for fun. She's hiding for her life. The fugitive dullness in her face, the animal lurch, the heat of her blood leaching into the air around us tell me: you are the world and I dread you. My name is being shouted from a hundred miles away. My brothers and my friends are calling me back to base, but I'm hearing only her labored breathing and the buzz of drowsy bees.

The light in the gloaming fades to violet, turning us to ghosts in the cotton. We don't move. We don't hazard a look away for a second. I'm eleven and I've never seen anyone like her. She's strange and beautiful in her dread. She looks to be fourteen or so because already I can see breasts pushing through her blouse and her cut-offs show her long smooth legs annealed by summer sun. She's poor, the child of a hungry household, and she's crossed the shallow Rio to make a new life here. I wonder what she thinks of me. I'm almost as dark, my hair as black, and my name comes from across the Rio too, but everything else says I live a settled untroubled life. Nothing fugitive about me. I'm the American she hates and hopes to be, and I can bring ruin on her just for being here. I see that apprehension pass over her face. She stirs. Moving with slow feline care, she swivels and creeps through the cotton into the next rut, making no sound at all. And just like that, the girl vanishes. I sit for a moment to ponder this apparition of my desire. All the prior times I came into the cotton, I came to dream myself to peace, and sometimes I dreamed a girl for company. I would talk with her. I would tell her stories. Before I even knew what desire was, I would sit with her and feel her warmth against mine. And now this girl appears, and she's like nothing I imagined. I think I should leave, I think I should run back to a hiding game that's probably all done by now.

But I follow her. I hold my breath again and wade through the welter of bolls and leaves and she's there. This time naked. Her brown naked back to me, she undoes her hair and lets it fall long, loose and black down her sloping shoulders. I see the fleshy curve of one breast when her arm is raised. Seeing the girl in this terrible intimacy scares me as something about the moment marks it all at once miraculous and forbidden. Like if I stare too long, I'll die or become a stalk of dumb cotton. She puts on a tee-shirt, then a light jacket, then quickly slips her legs into a long charcoal linen skirt, and I'm thankful for it. She must know this because she's aware of me now. She turns her head to confirm my presence as she shoves her wet clothes into the tote and puts on a floppy hippie hat in the style of the day. Her breathing calmer now. She raises her eyes to give me a look of confused pity that excites and devastates me. She parts her lips as if to say something but doesn't. That's all right. I know that already she dreads the world a little less.

I hear a motor turning in the coming darkness. A searing yellow light blazes through the field, skirting the upper edges of the crop. It's a Border Patrol cruiser throwing its searchlight into the cotton. The fugitive dullness falls over her face while my stomach churns with panic. I gaze for a second into the long, panning beam, and when I look back to the girl, she's not there. I look for her in the jungle of stems and leaves and across the ruts to the left and right, but she's gone. Or maybe turned to cotton. The bullhorn voice of *la migra* blares out garbled commands to come out, but I lie face-down in my rut to wait them out. They'll go soon. They'll give up their game and drive away, and I'll get up and go inside and eat my dinner and tell no one where I go to hide and seek.

LA LLORONA

I SAW HER.

Who.

La llorona.

No mames.

It was her. Swear to God.

We're playing this game, Kino, Marcos, and me, Michael and his little bro David, my brothers and my little sister too. Something involving the Sun Shopper. The thin tightly rolled weekly advertising rag that appears on our lawns every Thursday. We collect as many as we can and use them as weapons as we ride our bikes up and down the sidewalk in front of our *chante*, laughing and yowling, playing at gladiators till it's so dark we can't see faces, only our bicycle reflectors and the soiled white of our tees.

It's Demon who says it. Standing in the grass looking south on Polo Inn Street. Though we can hardly see him, we know him from his height, from the shape of his head, from the odd halting walk he's adopted for the street. We find ourselves walking our bikes toward him with the kind of trance-like apprehension only kids know, looking where Demon is looking, down this dark street on an evening where everything is pitched blue and black except the pale ice of the stars.

I saw her.

Are you sure?

Es la llorona, he says, like he wishes he hadn't. Actually, I'm not so sure he did. The words sound like they came out years ago, before Demon was Demon.

What does she look like, *ese*?

No sé. But I know it was her.

Did she say anything?

She made this sound.

We wait and listen for the sound. Looking in the dense tree-lined shadows of Polo Inn Street, which runs past Cowboy Park and the dried-up irrigation ditch and the older crumbling houses of the last half-century all the way to the Rio Grande, where already they are laying the groundwork for the Border Freeway, we listen for the call of *la llorona*. We don't know what *la llorona* is, nor what she signifies, not even what her call might sound like, but we know it can't be good.

You wanna go see?

I will if you will.

Pos, vamos.

I straddle my bike and pedal in with some of the others, including Demon in his blocky shoes, while the younger ones hang back to watch from a safe distance. We feel brave like little shits sometimes can, armored with the insistence inside us that says we're too old to be fooled now. Stepping into this long soundless street where the darkest of nights might be chiseling out some legend of our *abuelas'* imaginations; that's just another game for us to play. But then, wait.

Híjole, is that someone . . . ?

Did you see that . . . ?

What is that?

Like a person standing in the street. She seems to be waving something. A light appears behind this figure and it turns into headlights and the headlights brighten and dim according to the levels of reality that spill from our crazy heads. They seem to come directly toward us at a fast clip, then stop about fifty yards away, throwing more unsettling light in our eyes. We move to the gravel shoulder and wait for whatever to pass, but it just sits there for a long minute. And not a sound from it, either. The lights blink off, blink on. We speculate on what that means. Is it a drug deal? A *coyote* picking up some tired *mojadito* who just came across? A fight between lovers? A kidnapping, maybe? Before we can make up our minds about anything, the figure appears again silhouetted in front of the lights, startling us, and it or she or whatever hovers there for a moment, until the lights go into reverse and fade out completely. After that, nothing. We're weirded out by this mystery of lights and figures, but just when we think we've seen the end of it, the end of it comes. This thin faraway cry.

Was that a dog?

I don't think so.

It sounded like laughing.

No way.

Somebody crying.

Coulda been a radio.

No mames.

I think I want to go back.

Let's just see, I say. It's probably nothing.

We take a few unsteady paces toward what was there before. I'm listening hard for the reed song of the cricket in the little ditch along the road but no. Not even the rustling of leaves. Up ahead, there's nothing I can see except the dim lights of houses in the far distance. Then, unbidden, some compulsion catches hold of me and the others at exactly the same time. Not another step taken. Not a word exchanged. 'Cause right then, right at this moment, we see it, we know it, this cavernous hole that extends all the way to the border levee and beyond, this unseen, unnamable airless nothing; Polo Inn Street, where a speeding truck that didn't stop left a broken-backed carcass where my dog used to be, where a thousand ghosts left a trail of cold river water as they made their way to a better, worse life, where a police cruiser with its lights off slowly rode the margins of some secret uncommitted crime, where a thick tongue bellowed in some house out there of sins older than God, when God was still a Mexican;

it's our own personal, lonely, designated hour staring back at us and there ain't shit to do or say about it except . . .

You know what? I'm hungry.

You know what? Me too.

Let's go inside.

Yeah.

And we turn back to our own *chantes* and sit at our proper sides of the table, watch our shows, share the jokes and stories of the day, except this mystery on *pinche* Polo Inn Street, before we head for baths and beds, and thereby soak up the vivid and visible life we know for as long as we know it.

It had to be a dog, anyway.

WILD KINGDOM

HE FIRED HIS GUN AT us but not 'cause he wants us dead. How could he? He's our dad. The same Dad who took us to Ruidoso every summer for some fresh mountain air and got us new bikes for Christmas. The same Dad who loves the Flip Wilson Show and croons along to Lucha Villa on the radio. But something's collapsing inside him for sure and lately he's a tense brooding man walking around the house with his hands clenched around some invisible giant rubber band. He's still our dad, though. Our *apá*.

We're supposed to be quiet in the afternoons, 'cause he's working six nights a week at this local greasy burger joint and he needs to sleep days. He's not so good when he's roused. He bellows for us to shut the hell up if we even pad down the halls too loud, and once he threw his shoe at my little brother and caught him right at the temple and almost knocked him out. So today we figure we'll watch some TV with the volume low. We're all sitting around watching Mutual of Omaha's Wild Kingdom. But my mom's not happy about something. She's all knotted up and tight-lipped, chewing on a fingernail while the jackals nip at the wildebeest carcass. She suddenly charges into the room where he's sprawled on the bed and snarls something nasty about him coming home later than he's supposed to, and smelling of drink on top of it, and he mutters something back, which results in *Amá* slamming the door and marching to the kitchen where she proceeds to wash the dishes as noisily as possible. He calls for her again after a while and she stomps back to him. We hear them yelling in the room. My brothers and me ignore the episode as best as we can, but we're quietly wishing we were out with our sister at Ascarate Park riding the cheap roller-coasters. It looks like it's gonna be another bad night.

Then the rubber band snaps and *Amá* sprints right through the house yelling for us to run. *¡Córrele! ¡Tiene la pistola!* With hardly a second to think about it we're all scrambling to our feet and dashing after her as we hear pop! pop! pop! I'm the last one out and just as I reach the door, I catch sight of a man I've never seen before, in tee-shirt and boxers, hair mussed up, glowering like a *Lucha Libre* wrestler, and in his hand, one of the guns that he keeps hidden in his closet. As he fires off one more POP! I fling myself out the front door, swearing there's a bullet searing into the small of my back but it's only fear burning there. Fear and exhilaration that we're out of the house unharmed. I think my mom's almost laughing, she's so scared.

In stupefaction, Diana and Joe from next door come out to find us crouched behind their station wagon. The other neighbors from across the street have also decided this escapade is better than Wild Kingdom. A few minutes later, the *Chota* pull up with no less than five cruisers with five cops looking at the front door of our *chante* with their five thumbs on the butts of their big black shiny pistols. One officer comes over to get the story from my mom. He has a mustache like my dad's. The door of my house opens up a crack and I hear this stranger croak out, It's over. I put the gun away. You can come back now. Whose voice is that? So broken, so clogged with misery and fatigue. I'm wondering if this is where the police blow him away. This is how these barrio stand-offs usually end. The officer with the mustache wants to know if he means to fire his weapon again. My mom shakes her head, but she can't chew the doubt off her fingernails. He can see it too. So he turns to me with a questioning look that shames me to the core. I want to explain to him the deal, I want to jump ahead twenty years for the words to say, maybe it's 'cause he hasn't slept so good in months, or maybe this job serving drunks and whores greasy food all night long doesn't pay for shit, or maybe he's realized at last that he's had five kids in five years by the time he's twenty-three with a woman who deserves better than she's getting and all the manhood dreams he conceived for his life are over for-fucking-ever, 'cause he's caught in a country that won't cut him a break except maybe to clean the toilets for the next shift and no last-ditch scramble back across the border is going to raise his prospects in any way. Too late for that. So what if he has a few on the way home, so what if he's tired and surly these days and so what if he took his gun out of his closet and shot off a couple rounds? He wasn't aiming for us. No way, *ese*. All the bullet holes are drilled into the floor, like he meant to miss, like he was only killing off our shadows. Maybe it's his own damn shadow he was really shooting at. Maybe the real crime happened a long time before this and maybe another one's going to happen as soon as five thumbs get the notion. I know these out-of-range words are waiting for me and my father sometime in that more clear-headed day to come, but the present twelve-year-old little shit just stands there whimpering like a fool who wants his dad back.

The officer nods and walks calmly to the front screen door of my house and they talk for a while. Mustache to mustache. Then he turns to his fellow officers and gestures that it's okay and waves *Amá* over. Timidly to the door she goes and the three of them cluster in private conference until she steps inside. Then the officer walks away and just like that, the cruisers cruise away, the neighbors return to their homes, my brothers go back in the house for whatever comes after Wild Kingdom and the tired old sun slumps behind the Franklin Mountains.

I'm still standing by the station wagon, wondering what happened to my shadow.

OUR BLACKIE

BLACKIE IS OUR DOG. A handsome German shepherd with the most playful disposition. A stupid, happy, untrained dog who wears his tongue on the side of his mouth like a scarf. A dog house, a collar and a long chain attached to it are his. All the grass in the half circle of his perimeter in the backyard is gone, all dirt, all his. He is always barking, always pulling against the chain to be with us, to play with us. Always breaking it and leaping over the fence to run all over and befoul other neighbors' yards. He's never easy to catch, but we manage to get him every time. He drinks with huge sloppy bursts that spatter water all around and he eats like a bear. He is our playmate when we play Star Trek, we the crew of the *Enterprise*, Blackie the otherworldly creature. At night he is our sentry, warding off prowlers and cats when my dad is at work. When I am hurting, he is all the company I need and he lays his head across my lap to confirm it. His bark is fearsome, but we know it's how he beckons for love. Please, *please* let me play with you.

This is a *retablo* of our dog. He taught me about death.

He gets out of the backyard, squeezing past someone's legs at the gate, maybe mine. We try to catch him but he runs from us, throwing himself into the freedom of a larger world without chains or backyards or limited smells. His lolling red tongue is almost as long as his tail. He's in the full delight of his being. How can he see the pickup truck roaring up the road, how can he know that it's stronger than him, how can he foresee the pain it will bring in one thunderous crash, and how can he know that his spine is no match for the unforgiving impact in the bright Sunday light? There he is in the seconds he has left, lying in the gravel, struggling to move, his back visibly growing a new bone, and his happy dog face swelling with blood and all of us gathered around him like a campfire story we haven't heard yet. We watch him slowly become something other than dog something greater than our pet all the happiness draining from his eyes and filling up with a new mystery some deep new secret about us it's about us this dawning this world on the other side of our breathing where Blackie is now absorbed completely in one final gasping jolt while Kino and Marcos and my brothers cry openly and I think I should join them but I can't. I can't look at this thing anymore that used to be my dog so I go inside and turn on the TV and what is there but Lassie.

EL MERO MERO

WHAT THE HELL IS A man, anyway? I had a clearer sense of what that whole deal meant when I was a little *mocoso*, when everyone was older and taller and deeper-voiced than me and kept the Modelo Negro at arm's length. But now I'm growing some fine hair on my lip and my balls, my voice is dropping, and my flared jeans are all high-waters. I'm an easy target for my buds at the schoolyard. When's the flood comin', *ese*? It doesn't help that over my platform shoes, I'm often wearing white tube socks. Girls are kinda not into that. Clearly, I'm missing something.

But my *jefe*, my old man, my father. He's a man. He's got the forearms to prove it. He's modeled his squint after Charles Bronson and puts spicier *chile* on his eggs than anyone in our house. He busts his ass slinging burgers over spitting grease nine hours a day for us and doesn't ever complain about it. Then he comes home a drained man, dropping all the trappings of his day into the top drawer of his dresser before he drags himself into the shower. That's where all the talismans of manhood are kept.

Right now, he's not home. My mother is snoring on the couch while the six o'clock news blasts out of the Magnavox. Everyone else is either out or out of sight. It's like some muse of my adolescence is saying, Here's your chance, *baboso*.

Peering into his drawer, I take inventory of the tokens that make Dad Dad. His tin of *Pomada de la Campana*, some cologne in a boot-shaped bottle, shoe polish for his work Oxfords, a few ragged *pesos*, tangles of man bracelets, old watches and chains, random pens collected from various customers, some old keys, a pack of Camels, an engraved silver lighter and a single copper-headed bullet. These are the trinkets of my dad's personal mythology, all jumbled together with the carelessness of a working man.

Recalling how he applies the *pomada* on his fryer grease burns, I rub some on my hands and I douse my neck and face with his cologne, which burns into my raw pimples. I slick my hair back with his hair cream. Then I put the cross that he keeps on a gold chain around my neck, unbuttoning my paisley shirt down to my sternum so it shows, then try on one of his dead watches. Finally, I look at the structure of my new self in the mirror. *El mero mero*. The real-real.

El mero mero slinks out of the house and goes around to that derelict field where the cotton used to grow to shoulder height. He leans against the wall by the sere clumps of tumbleweed and breathes in his newfound musk. He looks down at the cross catching the sundown light. He rattles the bracelet around his skinny wrist as he raises a cigarette to his lips and lights it with his beautiful lighter. Oh, the sound of that lighter. Suppressing a cough, he looks out toward the blue-grey silhouette of the mountains in Ciudad Juárez where he imagines all the real men of the world are nodding their somber heads in unison at the spectacle of his arrival. *El mero mero*.

A group of three slouchy *vatos* in white tee-shirts and baggy khakis, old enough to drive a car but not old enough to own one, stroll down the street on their way to someplace better than where they were. *El mero mero* turns his gaze their way and they must feel it 'cause one of them looks right back at him and sneers *¿Qué ves, puto? El mero mero* looks away and that's when he hears them laughing. Not even very loud, not even with much derision, just the kind of laughing that diminishes a guy, the kind of laughing that flattens the sunset and puts it out of reach and causes all the fine hairs of a person like *el mero mero* to wish themselves onto some other body, not his. Little flecks of shame and anger swarm over him, and he doesn't even finish the Camel. *El mero mero* knows he'll slink back inside and put his old man's bracelet and cross, his crumpled pack of cigs and silver lighter back in the drawer and he'll wash off the *pomada* and cologne in the shower along with everything that makes him *el mero mero*. Except that in the little pocket of my high-water flared jeans that I'll wear for another humiliating month in a year of humiliating months, I'll keep a shiny copper-headed bullet for the day when I understand the real-real.

NOTHING HAPPENS

WHAT GOOD IS A STORY if nothing happens in it, if you don't know what the hell is even going on, not just in your school, your city, your country, but in your own damn thirteen-year-old heart where you feel but can't make sense of the same vibrations of rage and frustration buzzing in everyone else's head like guitar feedback, like the droning cicadas of the waning summer of 1970, tying knots in our throats till we spit them out as words we didn't know before like *Raza* and Az-tlán and MEChA and especially *Chicano*, which is something you suddenly are, someone different from your parents, distinct from them by birth and earth, a new species of American with a sense of purpose forged out of our common brownness and out of the crime you're hearing on the news about Rubén, Rubén our brother killed in *Califas*, one of our own, born in Juárez, raised in El Paso, now working for the *prensa* in LA, now dead, killed at a rally broken up by the cops, which is why we're marching for him, your buddies say, we're gonna walk out of school on Monday and march for Rubén, and they ask you if you're marching on Monday too and all you say is I gotta ask for permission, but your mother says, *Oye*, don't you dare miss your classes, no skipping school, and your father warns, I better not see you on TV, 'cause he knows the revolution will be televised but you tell them you'll be live on the six o'clock, you're that high with your thirteen-year-old's rebellion, your buddies too, all high on the weekend's anticipation until Monday comes, the buzz inside you getting louder as you start to see it in others, the anticipation of *la marcha*, the glory of revolt like fire ants in their eyes, even as Principal Dorgan says over the intercom anyone walking out will be marked as truant, but we're going anyway, even this girl I like and her friends are going, only the goody-goody ones staying, but not you, the lunch bell declares, not fucking you, as you head down the hall toward the big glass doors when this nausea hits you with a thousand questions, like are some of them walking out just so they can ditch classes for the rest of the day, do they care what the cause is, do they know enough about solidarity to protest, get arrested, maybe even killed by some damn tear gas canister, don't they just wanna smoke Salems and drink Blue Nun by the river, and what if most of them are really going into the streets with the heat in their hearts for Rubén and what if this is the moment that defines not just an era but a whole people and what if this is your defining moment, will you miss out on that or do you think that by not walking out you're making your own statement about how to move the cause forward and do you really believe that 'cause you might be saying that so you don't feel so chicken-shit, all these questions, dirty questions detouring you back to your locker to your notebook to your social studies class, where nothing happens to you sitting alone with the teacher except the buzz turns by increments to subtle tonalities of shame, while you throw a longing look out the louvered window where some better part of you, a real *Chicano*, is marching for Rubén Salazar? So what good is a story if nothing happens but that?

EL KITTY

MY SISTER IS FIFTEEN IN her hippy blouse and maxi skirt squinting into the Polaroid lens as she stands in our carport on the first day of school, her smile weighed down by some vague apprehension, maybe some inkling of the blitzkrieg that adolescence will rain down on us, or some remnant of earlier turmoil, a secret that an only daughter in a family of boys might harbor. I see her with that plastic flower in her hair and the light on her so splendidly diffuse, the way sunlight always appears in recollection. *Se ve tan triste, mi carnala*, and it's a sadness she plies admirably today, annealed as it is in her face by the processes of time, work and childbirth into something sturdy and defiant, which is how we're able to bear our inner trials.

All those days she took care of us are the catalogue of her grace, and it's these that reveal the more complex image of her. Younger by two years but older than me in every way, she plays the parent while the parents work. On these childhood afternoons she's there holding us safe in the aura of her soothing voice, her tender remonstrations, her radar wary over three unruly brothers storming the house with their Hot Wheels race cars and the orange tracks they ride on. She lays our little pink fingers on her lap and with a needle coaxes the splinters out; she presses bags of ice against the throbbing purple acorns on our foreheads while she sings us *sana sana colita de rana / si no sana hoy, sanará mañana*; she crawls under the bed with us when we're scared of thunder and thundering fathers, counting the seconds between each clap of the storm until it's a game for drawing our fears further off.

One of these games between us rises out of real grief. We have a cat, a tomcat I adopted but never really tamed, and he roams the neighborhood at will. He'll be gone for weeks then turn up mean and hungry on the porch, except for the one time he's gone for more than two months. When he finally appears on our doorstep with a leg completely stripped of fur and swollen raw with pus, we know it's not for food. My father calls Animal Control, who takes him away and that's as much as I need to know. But somehow, in the containment of my sorrow, in the kind of miracle that only dumb nine-yearold kids dream up, I become the Kitty and my sister obligingly takes on the Mommy. I curl my little brown fists into paws and lick them for her. I meow. I crawl on all fours to cuddle and be cuddled. I soften my voice and pitch it high like a cartoon while hers is soothing, unmistakably maternal. Our brothers also play with her like this, but for me, it's a special relationship built on the intimacy of loneliness and loss.

We play before bed and under the table and on the car drives to the Big 8 Grocery Store. We play in the closet among the musty shoes and old relics of Mamá Concha and in the backyard tree where the cicadas drone all day like lawn mowers. Games of primordial childhood in which I play at misbehavior and she scolds me, games of tickling and games in which we make up songs together, simple, private jingles that stumble forth from our little mouths to smooth the serrated tensions of a silent house.

Meorr.

Kitty.

Meorr.

Kitty, come.

Mama mad.

I'm not mad. I want to pet you.

Meorr.

You been good?

Uh-huh.

You had a bath already?

Uh-huh.

Let me see your paw.

No.

Let me see it.

No.

Why not?

'Cause.

I won't hurt you.

Meorr.

Oh, you have a splinter. Let me take it out.

Meorr.

See? It didn't hurt. I'll give it a *besito* to help it heal.

Meorr.

Silly thing. I always take care of you.

We start this when we are too young to know what young means, when the candles on our cakes seem longer than our fingers. Now, as we grow older, we play less and less, but whenever things are fraught and I start gnawing at my fingernails and even the skin around them, she gently pulls my hand away from my mouth, folds it into a paw and whispers

Kitty.

And Kitty comes back.

Early one languorous Saturday afternoon, I hear music coming from her room, and I find her sprawled on her bed on top of the covers, looking up at the tiny crystal glints in our popcorn ceiling, caught in Roberta Flack's contemplation of the first time ever she saw that face. The blinds are closed against the jarring sun. Her hands drawn up to the base of her neck. She's hardly aware of me at the doorway. I creep in on my hands and knees and crawl up next to her, take her hand and purr into the crook of her neck. Giving my hand an imperceptible squeeze, she permits herself the thinnest sigh, as if to blow some trouble off her lip.

Meorr.

She scarcely blinks.

Meorr.

The tiny pulse in her neck bounces to the bass line in the song.

Meorr.

I look at her profile and find that something in Roberta's voice has balanced a tear on the lashes of one eye. Anything more, even for a girl of eleven, would cheapen the heartache. But instead of leaving her to her study, I let the Kitty purr. It's my turn to offer solace to my sad *carnalita* with a playful tap of a ghost cat's paw.

Meorr.

In one sweeping gesture, she pushes my hand away, sits up and turns a scowl on my Kitty face. When are you going to quit this? When are you going to grow up? *No eres el Kitty. Ese gato ya se murió.*

She slaps on her shoes with a brusqueness new to me and leaves the room, like she just remembered something more important. The song isn't even over. Roberta drones on. But the cat is dead. It died years ago. One day I might thank my sister for this exorcism, for sloughing off the last bits of our stale *infancia*, but for the moment I kneel by her bed feeling the burn in my ears spread over my face as I uncurl my paw and inspect my ravaged fingers.

LOCURA

IT'S ALL ABOUT THE BANANAS, really. I see her at our first meeting of the Drama Club in September. Frisky freshman girl, blood high in her cheeks, sparkling eyes. Her name is Valentina and for a long time after, I'll always associate that name with the kind of longing that turns otherwise sensible boys into fools. 'Cause without even having a word with her, I tell myself she's the one.

She's got other ideas, though. With the deftness of a girl who's already had to deal with a ton of homeboy crushes, Valentina gently tempers the fires of this skinny brown kid. She's pleasant and warm, but not warm enough to warrant any hopes of something deeper. In little notes painstakingly composed and perfumed with the musk of my want, I launch my heart across the room at her. But they hardly elicit anything more than a genial smirk and a shrug.

Instead of letting it go, what I do like an idiot? I gather up all my hurt into this nasty little fixation and suck it up like a drug. All the rest of that year, I'm throwing her sad *cholo* looks that say, I do it all for you.

Then come these black moods that I fall into like manholes. I grow moody and taciturn. Every day is dusk. Something's off inside of me for sure, *pero ¿qué?* I make up symptoms that cry for some diagnosis. Like losing the feeling in my right hand. I drop notebooks, pencils, paper cups, usually stuff that won't break or spill on people. I develop a new kind of schoolboy amnesia, where I conveniently forget the names of teachers, homework, simple tasks. At work, Cisco thinks I'm hitting some really strong pot. My drama coach wonders if puberty is making a late hello. My friends think it's an arty affectation. I don't know the word languor yet, so in my head I call it *Locura*.

What does Valentina think? How does she react to my afflictions? With complete indifference. It's like she knows I'm the star of my own private soap and it doesn't matter if she's in it. Sometimes I think I almost see concern glance across her face. Other times, she seems bemused. Maybe she knows how it ends in bananas.

A few years before all this, down in the village of Nazas deep in northern Mexico, exploring my grandparents' crumbling old house, we stumbled on a family secret in one of the back rooms. An uncle hidden from the world. He'd been called up for military service but took a bad fall during his training and apparently landed on his head. They sent him home to recover, but he was never the same. They kept him in that dank empty room like a sick animal and fed him bananas. We saw him shoving bananas in his mouth. All his life bananas. Our first glance at *Locura*.

Almost a year goes by. There's a big dance at the school and I know Valentina will be there. I stride all *firme* into the gym where the streamers are hanging and buy a cup of soda with ice. The lights alternate red, green and white on the basketball court. The discothèque music boom-booming off the ceiling. All the girls in their tight dresses. I got my best duds on, clip-on bow tie, platform shoes, a good dab of Brut cologne on my neck and armpits. Shiny watch on my left wrist, *Locura* on my right. And directly before me is Valentina in her mini-skirt and heels talking with her friends. Soon as I'm in her line of sight, my cup of soda slips out of my hand and splashes onto the floor. Instead of showing concern for the haywire nerves in my hand, everyone snorts and thinks what a dumb klutz.

But *Locura* does an encore. In the next beat, there's a

wavering of speech, an unbuckling of joints, then a tumble to the floor. I feel the bass-beat pulsing against my face as all these bell-bottom pant-legs and bare kneecaps encircle me. I make my tongue go numb. My limbs go slack. I let my vision blur, except for the split second it takes to look for Valentina. She's not there, though. I reel around and scan for any sight of her by the soda stand, the DJ station, the bathroom line, but in a moment, it's all crowded out by the back-lit heads of the teacher-chaperones. I hear them asking if I'm drunk. Someone smells my breath. Someone says, Call his parents.

A few more boom-booming numbers later, I feel her standing over me. Not Valentina, but Mom. I know it's her, I can make out her wrenched face in the dark, and yet I make myself forget, and in my quavering voice, I say, *Amá*? Is that you? She sobs once and tightly clenches me to her chest. Some of the guys hoist me to the car. Everyone distressed but not as much as I thought. I hear them in the dark outside.

He was fine a few minutes before, *señora*.

I thought he was going to throw up on me.

He just needs to sleep it off.

It was nice knowing you, *vato*.

They bring me home and put me to bed. I lie there sweating into the pillow. Inexplicably, Valentina is a thousand miles from my mind. I don't want to her to know what happened. I don't even want to think about the shit I just pulled off. I'm more interested in what they're saying on the other side of the door, my parents, the whole family.

What's wrong with him?

Maybe he was drinking.

Maybe someone slipped something in his Coke.

Like what? Liquor? Whiskey?

That or maybe a drug.

Ay pobrecito mijo. He didn't even know me.

What if he's gone psycho?

Ay Diosito. ¡Ojalá que no!

What if he's faking?

Why would he do that? *¡No seas estúpido!*

Should we take him to the hospital?

Are we locking him in his room from now on?

Are we going to feed him bananas every day?

Every day? *¡Chale!* We can't do that. Bananas are expensive.

It could happen. This *Locura*, if I'm being honest, is only love. But who wants to be honest? I put on the best acting performance of my life for the attention of this girl who wasn't even there to see it. *Locura* and I fooled everyone, but now here I am about to live out my life like my poor idiot uncle. In a diaper sitting in one corner of the empty room and in the opposite corner a mass of banana peels piled all the way up to the ceiling. Here comes Mom with my breakfast. *Buenos días, mijo. Mira*, your favorite: *Choco-Milk y* bananas.

Next morning before everyone is up, I take a shower and go for a run at the track at school. Cured of my *Locura*. All my infatuations, all my disorders, sweating them off in a few laps. In their place, feelings of embarrassment and relief that I didn't cause more harm than I did. Thankfully, they hardly even mention the episode when I get home.

More than three years on, at the frazzled end of a long college night, sitting drunk and alone in my dorm room, I come across her fragile teenage cursive in the back of my high school yearbook:

Please forgive and understand me but I was too young to realize the beautiful friendship I was going to lose. Believe me, now I understand it all and I regret treating you the way I did with all my heart. I guess you can say I barely grew up. . . .

Exactly the words that I should have conveyed to her. *Pinche Locura.*

JEEP IN THE WATER

THE RIO GRANDE WE CALL it on the US side. Río Bravo is what they call it in Mexico. The difference is the difference. Somewhere in the murky depths of this beleaguered band of water is a demarcation line invisible to all but the respective governments of both nations.

One morning a long time ago, which in El Paso could mean either fifty years ago or yesterday, two Border Patrol field agents on their rounds spot a dealer-fresh cherry-red Jeep parked in the shallow Rio. It sits unattended right in the center, the brown water coursing halfway up the doors, loaded with kilos of marijuana. Upon inspection, the agents surmise that some audacious drug runners from Juárez somehow got it into their *cabezas* that if they had the right vehicle, they could simply drive through the river at its shallowest point and safely transport their cargo to its destination. It almost worked. They probably felt like geniuses as their Jeep readily churned through the water in the dead of night. But right at midstream with no horses to jump to, the Jeep had come to a gurgling halt, mired in deep silty sludge. The dried spatters of mud on the shiny red exterior suggest to the agents some recent desperate heaving back and forth of the vehicle. Apparently, the deflated smugglers abandoned their mission and waded back to Juárez, sans Mary Jane.

Pleased with their catch, the Border Patrol field agents notify their superiors and summon a tow truck to drag the Jeep to shore. By now, a small crowd of people has gathered on both sides of the river to gawk, alerted to the spectacle by the traffic choppers of morning radio. The congregations seem harmless enough, more bemused than alarmed at the sight of a stranded Jeep in the middle of the river, so the agents take only standard cursory notice.

The tow truck appears on the scene in due time and the young attendant begins running a long tow line to the Jeep. That's when things take an ugly turn. Before he can reach the vehicle, he's being pelted by the Juárez assembly with stones, slabs of concrete, bottles and whatever else is handy, and he is driven back out of the water. The agents shout admonitions to the suddenly bristling mob, but at that moment a tow truck on the Mexican side backs up to the bank and two men charge into the river with their own tow line. This brazen act affords some incentive to the Border Patrol tow man, and he barrels back into the water. An uproar of curses rises from both side of the river in two languages as the men slosh like lunatics to the Jeep with their tow lines. The Mexicans secure theirs to the rear fender of the Jeep while the American ties his to the front. Then the contest begins.

The tow trucks rev their engines, pull the tow lines taut, and proceed to pull on the Jeep in opposite directions. An international tug-of-war commences with great noise and cheering from the gathered spectators, many of them already picnicking on the promontories with churros and beer. Back and forth lurches the Jeep, first toward Mexico, then toward the US, then back Mexico-way. Wagers are taken on who will prevail. Some brave boys even grab the line and tug hard to stack the odds in Juárez's favor. The Border Patrol fire warning shots in the air to disperse the crowd and demand the tow-truck desperados cease their criminal acts, but it's no use. Nobody can hear the shots above the shouting and the clamor of the news choppers directly overhead. This is now a full-blown international incident.

At long last, a larger heavy-duty tow behemoth designed for hauling eighteen-wheelers pulls up to the US embankment, and its seasoned driver, long in the tooth and short in the saddle, dodging various projectiles, succeeds in attaching his own tow line to the derelict Jeep. Once ashore, he climbs into his cab and sets to towing it out of the water. The crowds fall silent as the steel cable tautens. *Señor* Jeep heaves mournfully for a moment over the loud grind of the overheating engine of the Mexican tow truck. Then a hideous crunch is heard as the rear fender snaps off and flies into the air like a catfish being reeled in. To cheers from the Americans, and jeers from the Mexicans, the Jeep slowly taxis northward to America, but not before some daring half-naked Mexican kids rush to snatch some bags of pot, souvenirs of this mighty Pan-American match.

The Jeep is impounded, the marijuana seized, displayed and destroyed, and the story, widely circulated for a time throughout the Southwest with many a chuckle, is eventually forgotten in the mix of more sensational and bloodier stories of the War on Drugs bedeviling the region.

But somewhere below the surface of this river, covered over by the silt of years like the footprints of an ancient dinosaur, lies the imprint of tire tracks from a solitary Jeep that challenged the legitimacy of this invisible line we call the Border.

SKINNY BROWN KID DOESN'T KNOW SHIT

A SKINNY BROWN KID DOESN'T know shit. He's lost in his own house. Lost in his dreams for a skinny brown girl. All his insides dissolving to mush. Secreted through his skin as longing. I'm sitting on the fence looking across the street at the houses with their lights on. The moon coming up half-eaten, the twilight bus lurching past like a sick elephant. I can't get the pictures out of my head. Cathy in the moors, Heathcliff dying in the dense nothing of his loss. The books I'm reading are lending all the credence I need.

Margaret O doesn't know me. She doesn't know how I feel. I tell her after English class but the words come out wrong, all jumbled up and wrong. I think I hold her hand once, I think I kiss her once, but I'm not sure any of it is real. I'm quoting lines from Annabel Lee, warning myself away from the evil taking hold of that vital organ I'd hardly known was there. I knew its steady thumping, but had thought it was only there to push blood through the veins of a skinny brown kid. Now I know it's for loving. That's the evil, the hurt that loving brings, the quiet broil in the chest that burns through the insulation of reason. Kills all your thoughts, sucks up all the things you used to like and drains them of need. A love that was more than love, Poe says.

I wander to the park where some Youth League ballgame is going on. My hands clench the chain-link fence. The floodlights are a comfort, the kids chanting batter-batter-batter-batter-batter, the parents yelling at the coach, the ice-cream truck dispensing soft-serve and sno-cones. Proof that the world goes on, that life is still mostly sport. But this skinny brown kid zeroes in on the Umpire. Tall and thick, dressed in black from head to heel, with a leather cage for a face. His Umpire voice is fierce and baleful, coarse as gravel. Strike! he cries, like a demand. Strike! like he's telling the batter to take a swing at me. Strike down that little fool for these grown-up degradations in his heart! And when he shouts Yerrrrrout! he makes that ripping gesture with his arm like he's eviscerating me, and the ketchup blotches on the pavement are signs to be read. All the signs saying no and no and not this time and no way, *ese*. This Umpirical black figure, who Catherine feared, who chased Poe through the streets of Baltimore, who set fire to Rochester's bed, who dared my hands toward the fuzz taking root in my groin. A foul ball slams against the fence at my face, and I gasp. The Ump scowls in my direction and pulls a fresh ball from inside his black chest. Foul! he cries.

I'm walking home through the soggy grass and I feel him behind me. I step inside my house and feel him in my backyard. He's looking in my window. I bury my face in the pillow and cry. O Maggie, Maggie O. What can I do? My insides turning to soup, all guts and hominy. The want taking over everything. The Umpire tapping on the pane says, You're up. I can't think, I can't feel anything but this evil. I can see through my shirt the skin and through the skin the pathetic little knot of tissue calling for her, Maggie, look at me hurt, look at me demeaned in the dark of my love for you, Margaret O, I'm dying. I find my dog-eared Brontë on the dresser. It's assigned to us for English I, but right now I'm reading it for Biology. I curl up in my preteen desolation, fever through the words written years and miles ago and locate the place of pain in the story. There are no moors in El Paso, I don't even know what moors are, but the Wuthering Heights are right here. Oh yes, right in here. A refuge, a sweet and fiery sanctuary for this skinny brown kid who doesn't know shit but is sure as hell learning it by heart.

SIREN SONGS

THE FERROUS TASTE OF THE air after a good rain is what I remember.

That and the sounds of frogs chirping in the sodden fields behind our house. In the fields and in the park with the swing set and the small trees glistening in the aftermath of a storm that barreled through the night before.

It's like the rain coaxed them out to sing. Like the earth became so saturated that it yielded up a crop of frogs overnight, with their reedy songs pre-empting the roosters at the first blue wink of dawn.

It's me and my brothers and the boy who's seeing my sister in the morning of some July, walking outside just as the last bank of clouds rolls off, and we're struck by this jangly chorus. It's a strange cacophony we've heard before but never so spirited this early in the day, never pitched with such ecstasy.

We follow the siren song to the park, the freshness of the morning air against our faces. It won't be long before summer heat grinds itself in. At the park, there's flooding everywhere, enormous pockets of rainwater all over the lawn reflecting the overcast sky above. And frogs everywhere. Fat grey muddy frogs of all sizes, sitting in the puddling like stones, their throats ballooned with amphibian *boleros*. They start slopping about when we come near, thrusting their long legs into the air, landing haphazardly on top of each other. It's an orgy of frogs and standing in the middle of it is Demon.

That's what we call him. One of the local kids, he's not

really a kid. He might be two years older, he might be ten, but he's shorter than us by almost a foot, and he doesn't talk much. His eyes are always bloodshot from the paint thinner he sniffs and his skin is bad, and his head is shaped like a baby's when it's fresh out of the womb. He looks like he could be dangerous, but not to us. With us, he's almost a child.

Demon is watching the frog dances around him with sullen detachment. Picking the largest frog in his perimeter, he takes out of his pocket a Black Cat for the Fourth of July and places it in its mouth like a cigarette. We start laughing. It's funny to see that frog with a firecracker in its mouth. Then Demon lights the greasy fuse and backs away and watches it explode. It's kind of horrible. But we laugh even louder. My sister's boyfriend takes a Black Cat from Demon and lights it on another frog and up it goes into the air, shredded to pieces. Then other kids come out with their firecrackers and soon there's a different kind of orgy. And everyone's laughing. All these dead frogs all over the park, and specks of mud and blood on our shirts and faces and we're laughing.

We go back to our house and sit around the porch and then we're quiet. Nobody's saying shit. I don't know why, like I don't know why we were laughing. Demon comes by and squats on his haunches. He sticks a cigarette in his mouth. He lights it and puffs out his cheeks as he lets out a long thin strand of smoke. In the distance, it's not the frog choir we hear but the constant pop pop pop of firecrackers. And the silence of the park for many summers after.

FIRST DAY

WE'RE IN HIS BUICK REGAL, letting the brassy noise on the ra
dio pass for conversation. Dad sitting high in his seat and me
slumped in mine. We haven't been close for some time. The
barrier between us is made of various compacted resentments
and coarse particles of dried emotional dung. But it can't keep
him from guessing what I think of his job. He's the day cook
at the locally famous taco joint on Montana Street. He's seen
the look on my face when he comes home reeking of fryer
fat and onions, his shirt smeared with ketchup, mustard and
burnedin lard. No following in the old man's footsteps for me.

Still, I need the job. My last gig delivering the *El Paso
Times* around the neighborhood didn't go so well. I kept over-
sleeping, finding flats on my bike, throwing the papers on the
wrong front porches and generally infuriating people. That
lasted a whole month and the cash I had to show for it didn't
amount to squat. Consequently, my route goes to another paper boy and I resign myself to the taco palace.

Several blocks away from the place, *Apá* turns the radio
down and rattles off some things I should know before going
in. Smile and stand up straight. Make sure your hair is neat
and combed and tuck your shirt in. Listen to the manager and
don't be afraid to ask questions. Above all, respect your customers. I know, I know, I mutter back, trying not to sound
whiny about it.

We arrive half an hour before opening and most of the
crew is there. Conchita *y* Maria, both of whom must be in
their mid-sixties, prep in the kitchen area, stirring the sauce

for the tacos and grating the cheese that goes on top. *Buenas, Tavo,* they call to my dad. In the front counter area, the manager Mr. Alarcon assiduously counts the bills in the register while the other four employees wipe down the counter and sweep the floor around the tables. My *apá* introduces me and everyone greets me with morning smiles and *mucho-gustos.* All the employees come in various shades of brown like me, except for the tall wiry light-skinned guy who wears his hair combed down over his brow like Paul on Abbey Road. Without pausing in his count, Mr. Alarcon assigns him to me.

Cisco, *enséñale cómo se hace todo.*

Cisco nods in that easygoing way that I'll learn is his trademark and tosses me an apron. Then he asks me, *¿Cómo te llamas?, ¿Junior o Tavo Jr.?*

He passes for a white kid from the West Side, but like the others, he's a recent import from across the *río* in Juárez. Something in the dusty blue of his eyes insinuates the Third World in his blood. Even with that Tiger Beat grin, he's entirely and indisputably *Mexicano.*

Ni uno. I tell him in my own broken Spanish that I'm neither a junior nor a Tavo. I want to be Octavio. That's how I'm known in school and what I want to be called at work.

Cisco chuckles with a knowing wink, slaps a paper hat on my head and proclaims: Time to work, Octavio.

We spend the first part of the morning going over the menu and the procedure for taking orders on my pad, then he trains me on the register. With the deftness that comes from years of working these fast food palaces, Cisco demonstrates how to put the food and drinks on the tray without spilling a drop on the napkins and little paper cups of *chile.* I've hardly thought to look toward the kitchen area, but I know Dad's watching me the whole time.

¿Qué pasó? he gruffly asks. You don't want to be Tavo Jr.?

He's at the service window in a spotless white shirt and

apron, looking like Omar Bradley in his crisp paper hat. He's relaxed, genially twirling the spatula like a baton, looking softer than I remember him at home. Not the stern and stoic father I've set my moat around.

I like Octavio better, Dad.

¿O sí?

Yeah, I think so.

Pues . . . He pauses, then nods. *Está bien.*

At 9:30, the manager moves on to the other branch and the first customers make their way through the door. My hands are shaking as I take down orders and I have to keep looking back at the lit-up menu for the prices, but I seem to be getting things right. More customers stream in as we hit the lunch rush, and suddenly everyone's racing around me, their fingers hitting the keys of the register at a speed I can't match, fixing their trays with such blurring ease, and through the service window, I see Maria and Conchita prepping and garnishing so crazy fast while *Apá* is flipping up to twelve patties of burger meat on the hot grill, and all of them get that raw glow of perspiration on their brows. Cisco and the others take turns calling order numbers on the microphone in their stiff border accents—number 26, number 26, 26 please, number 27, number 30—while walk-ins at the counter are bellowing demands—not so much ice on the Coke, no onions please, extra *chile por favor*, three bean burritos and two orders of tacos to go and still more crowds file in for their midday bite—number 56, number 57, 57 please—and I'm finally getting the hang of this thing, until I drop a whole tray of sodas on the floor and Cisco laughs and yells, Get a mop, Octavio! Number 89! Number 90! 91! Two men in work boots and sunburned arms stalk in and order twenty-five singles of tacos with the sauce on the side and eighteen cheeseburgers with fries to go and Letty who takes the order says, Tavo, can you do it? My dad looks at the slip and shakes his head like he's going to say no, but actually says yes, and looks at the two men and says it again so they hear it, Yes, we can do it. Now he's packing the grill with more patties than I've ever seen and putting pans on the stove to heat the buns on while the *señoras* in the back fix the tacos in their trays, and now he's really sweating, his shirt getting those small Rorschachs in the back and near the arms, and his hat slips to a more rakish angle as he slams a stack of frozen taters into the deep fryer and still the others shout his name: Tavo, we need more cheese on this, Tavo, this lady says she's in a hurry, Tavo, make that two double-cheeseburgers. Tavo burning his fingers on the grill, his Tavo face getting grease-spat by the fryer, Tavo shoving to-go bags under the heat lamp, it's ridiculous how soundly he works, without panic, without rancor, with the full-on poise of a West Texas short-order cook in one of the most enduringly popular taco spots this side of the Rio Grande.

At last, the crowd has thinned, the two men load their togo orders onto their pickup, and my dad cleans his grill with a worn black pumice brick as he orders Conchita and Maria to take their break. I'm dead on my feet already, trying to figure out how the time went from 11:30 to 2 so damned quick. Cisco not only managed to take more orders than anyone at the counter, but he also raked in a couple of girls' phone numbers too. *Mis girhfrens*, he says. He laughs at the soda and salsa stains all over my shirt and pants. I'm laughing too. Then he turns my attention to something going on in the back storage area. Conchita and Maria are clapping at the sight of my *apá* lifting the 500 lb. ice machine so that Letty can get her mop under it. His forearms swell till the veins show and he's red in the face, but he's beaming all the same. We are, too. Cisco, in his smooth Cisco manner, only cocks his head to ask me one more time.

¿Y ahora quién eres? ¿Junior o Tavo Jr.?

WORLD GOES AWAY

I'M IN DISBELIEF. I'M AT a loss to explain how I got here.

It's my first week as a sophomore, and instead of enjoying the afternoon watching TV and doing my homework at my leisure, I'm at the first reading of a play at my school. The Diary of Anne Frank. All these poor idiots sitting in a circle with me are wondering how they got here too, some of them pleased as punch, others with the same perplexed look that's plastered on my face. We're assembled in the auditorium, which also passes for the basketball court and gymnasium. Listening to our drama coach laying down the laws of daily rehearsal. Miss Griffing is a feisty West Texan, short and sturdy, with close-cropped hair and glasses, and she's calmly setting forth the hours and days we'll be working, and underscoring her expectations of us as actors. She's grinning all smug and shit 'cause she knows some of us will defy these expectations, for which she's got gallons of two-fisted fury saved up in her compact frame. For now, just her bearing is enough to keep us in line. All I'm thinking is, shit, my afternoons are shot to hell forever.

What's worse is that now she has us holding hands and bowing our heads for prayer circle. She's calling for Jesus to bless our production, assuring him that we're only here to do his will, even though the play is about Jews in Nazi Europe. I'm confused and dismayed as this cycle of prayer goes on for a full fifteen minutes, with other students chiming in their amens and yes-fathers. If this is going to happen every time we meet for play practice, then I'm done. I'm already suffocating with all this sudden godliness, all these rules, all the hours wasted in a cavernous gym with this tough-ass teacher crying hallelujah. I don't know how she managed to get me to agree to be in this show, but I'm shaking out of this obligation quick. I resolve to sit through this one session with as good an attitude as I can muster up but when it's over, it's over. I'm not coming back. Not even if I'm playing Peter Van Daan, one of the young leads in the play. I don't care. Let them find someone else.

Finally, with everyone ready and worked up on Jesus, we take our seats in the circle as Miss Griffing passes out the scripts. She reminds us who's playing what role and directs us to read loudly, with feeling and enunciation. That last word is new to me but it sounds pretty religious. We open the scripts and begin reading, and gradually with the first girl's voice taking on the words of Anne Frank, the physics in the room begin to change. I feel the voice of this dark long-haired Mexican schoolgirl peel away the walls of the gym to reveal wartime Amsterdam, and then I see Anne herself huddled with her diary in the secret attic of her tragic story. Within the empty space of the circle, other voices around me lay down the vivid action of the play with passion, energy and conviction and then it's my turn. Some impulse takes over and I'm not me anymore but Peter Van Daan aching for sunlight and a place of no fear and the love of a young girl. The words go in my eyes and come out my mouth with more heart than I thought I had, and in that moment, the school and the impossible classloads and the gangs that chase me on the way home and the Border Patrol and the tensions of home and my personal anxieties about who the fuck I am and all the lived experience that make my town this unspectacular, sporadically dangerous place simply go away. I am somewhere in the mind of a teenage girl who disappeared into the death camps, inhabiting her words like they're the only world that matters. When we get to the end, our Anne is openly crying as a mournful hush falls over us. I am bewildered. I want to know how this happened, how we made the world vanish for these few hours of reading.

After we stand and hold hands one more time for an adjourning prayer, Miss Griffing comes over to me while I'm gathering up my homework and getting ready to leave. She obviously senses my confusion. With my eyes on the script, I want to tell her it's a miracle, this play is a miracle, how it made all the people and things, all my cares and worries of my world, evaporate to nothing.

But she beats me to it, saying, Well. You're still here.

I look at her. I want to ask what she means.

She smiles that smug smile and goes to switch off the gymnasium lights, and I walk home in the dark. But I'll be back, script in hand, to find my heart again.

BAD BLOOD

HE'S THREE YEARS YOUNGER, BUT don't call him kid brother. It's late. Ten o'clock. My mother, she's crying, wailing to beat the band. My dad is sitting mopey and useless in his easy chair. What's wrong, I ask. He's run away from home, they say. He left because of what I said. I didn't say shit. But apparently, I did. I'm being quoted back word for word. Words like, Fool, what were you thinking. Words like, When are you gonna grow up. Words in Spanish like *pendejo* and *cabrón*. All that just for a traffic ticket he got in the family sedan. And now he's gone. Thirteen years old and gone. So now it's up to me to find him. My father puts on his jacket, gets the keys and out we go.

He can't be far. But maybe he is. I scan around for anything that moves. Old *borrachos* waiting by their cars to sober up. The stray dogs in their wanton quest for anything worth a raised leg. The sign on the storefront reads Bolt and Screw. That's what I'd like to do right now. But you know what? I brought this on myself.

Is that him there? With those other two little punks, hopscotching shadows and sucking on cheap cigarettes? I say, Pull over, and my old man does and stays in the car while I jump out and dash across the street straight for them. They break off in all directions, my brother sprinting behind an old grocery store long shut down and boarded up. I head him off on the other side and find him dangling from a chain-link fence, snared in the coils of barbed wire lining the top. Every move he makes puts the rooster tips on his back, his legs, his face. I yell at him to hold still and I'll help him get free, but he snarls something mean and tries to smash me in the face. I disentangle him and drag him back to the car by the scruff of his jeans jacket, yelling at him about Mom and what a dope he is and other incoherent crap. My dad sits there silently driving us back.

When we get home sometime around two a.m., my mom is ironing shirts, my father's shirts for work. She'd stopped crying sometime while we were gone, but she starts all over again when she sees the nicks on his face and arms. She says, Did you hurt him? I say, No, but what are you doing with those shirts? Your father needs them, she says. I turn to my brother and tell him to apologize for scaring our mother by running away from home. Instead, his face splits almost in half as he unloads on me the ripest angriest shit I've ever heard. Motherfucker. I hate you. I hate your fuckin ass. You're no brother to me. I say, You don't mean that. He says, I mean every word. You're nothing to me. I hate you, I'm done with your fuckin arrogant shit. I'm stunned at the force of his rage, all that invective streaming out of his mouth with such conviction. I tell him I love him. I say, I'm doing this for you, you jerk. But he says, Don't. Don't do me any favors. Just get the fuck out of my face. He's crying the whole time and I am too, if I'm honest. What have I done? Who put me in charge of my own kid brother? How am I gonna get him back? I reach for him and he spits, Touch me and I'll kill you, fucker. I wish you dead, so help me God! Get outta my face! Get outta my life! Fuck the fuck off! He stalks off on legs stiff with loathing to his room, where he proceeds to pound his fists through the walls and destroy his model airplane collection. I have specks of his blood on my fingers. My dad wipes a paw across his tired face and goes to his own room. My mother takes up her iron and presses steam into another shirt. The hoarse bilious shouting continues to barrel through the walls straight into my dreams. I'm standing there, looking down at those little

black specks thinking Jesus, let this day end, let it burn itself
out, tomorrow will be different, tomorrow will see us through.
Then I realize it's already tomorrow. This is tomorrow, the
first morning in what will be a decade of dead glances, bitter
stalemates and bad blood.

PENITENTE

THERE HE GOES. EVERY MORNING he passes by our house, walking that strange halting walk of the beaten-down to the Little Flower Church up the street. His back so bent he can see his old man shoes with every step. My mother tells me he volunteers at the church when he's not praying long hours. He polishes the saints, dusts the pews with a rag, sweeps and mops the floors, and at dusk hobbles back to his mom's house, from which he's apparently never moved out. In a few years, this *penitente* will be dead of complications from the injuries sustained at the plant where he worked and his obituary will pass unnoticed by most of the people who knew him.

Years ago, we were inseparable buds. Those were the times when I was still lost inside myself, as most acne-ridden teens are. I thought I needed some guidance and I thought he offered it. Two years older and two inches taller, he started coming around the house, mainly to catch a glimpse of my sister, who completely ignored him. It didn't stop him from leering at her whenever she went by. But I didn't care. I thought he was funny and wise about the ways of girls, and that wisdom was a faculty I profoundly lacked.

He believed disco was invented for him. He believed the music and the clubs and the culture of disco would get him laid for years. He bought piles of tight-in-the-crotch pleated slacks and slick rayon shirts with gaudy splashes of color. We'd sit in his room with the door closed and he would try on each of his shirts and make some disco moves to show how they draped and showed off his chest, and then he would brag about the size of his dick and his prowess with women. I never saw him with any girl, but I believed him because he was beautiful.

The one irritating thing about him, though, was the way he razzed me. He seemed to enjoy poking shit at me every chance he got, and he found my taste in music laughable, which let's face it, it was. Jim Croce and the Grassroots were my idea of hip. He also got a real charge out of my name, which he took through so many permutations until he settled on Hor, as in Hortavio. Hey Hor, he would say. You gotta stay out of the sun, *ese*. You want chicks to think you're black or what? I didn't know how to stand up to that shit back then. I told myself he didn't mean any of it. It was all for laughs.

He really fucked with me about my clothes, too. He said they were cheap. Cheap cotton, he said. His shirts were fine, silky to the touch. Feel, Hor, he said, feel the quality. The problem was quality didn't breathe. Five minutes on the dance floor and he was soaked. Still, to retain the drape of the fabric, he eschewed washing them, and sending them to the cleaners was out of the question. Who had the *feria* for that? Instead, he'd douse them in cologne and hang them in his closet to dry. Whenever we went out to the dances, he reeked of English Leather and stale sweat.

He credited these shirts with getting him a girlfriend. And through his intercession, I was introduced to her friend, who, in fact, became the first real girlfriend I ever had. We partnered a lot on double dates. We strolled along the church bazaars, went to the local dances. We made out on carnival rides at Ascarate Park and stamped hickeys on each other's necks. He showed us how to make the most of our Friday nights. Plus, he taught me how to do the hustle, which I practiced on the dancefloor of my bedroom every night, spinning like God on my axis.

That girlfriend dumped him, though, and he took it real bad. He called her all kinds of names and swore she'd phone him back for mercy, but mostly he just pined away, all flat-tire faced and blue. I remember him turning up the radio on that sad Chi-Lites song while he cried about how he missed her. So I guess he taught me about that shit, too.

I don't know how long we hung out, maybe hardly a year, but one day I was just done with him. I found him ridiculous. I found him insulting. I got tired of being called Hor. Every time he came by, I told my mother to say I wasn't there. But he wouldn't take the hint. He'd constantly phone me. He'd walk by my house and shoot his gaze through the gaps in the curtain. He got to be so annoying that one night I wished to God that he'd make him disappear from my life. It didn't matter that he was harmless. I didn't care that he was lonely and insecure. God, I said, do something about him. Days later, school started up and I didn't see him. For months. Then years. Anywhere. He was gone.

Decades came and went and so did I. All the lessons of my errant teens filed under So What. I'm someone else now and the town is another town to me, and "The Hustle" is an oldie with no air play. But there he goes, my inseparable bud, a sad misshapen penitent married to God's little house in the desert. I'm at a loss to understand. I don't believe in God, I'm not sure I ever did, so how can prayers forged in a young, unfinished heart lead to this? And how is it that now the penitent walking with his eyes on his old man shoes is me?

THE *QUINCE*

THIS IS MY FIRST *QUINCEAÑERA*. I have my tuxedo on with the frilly pink shirt and the oversize cufflinks. I have my shiny rented black shoes. And the boutonniere on my lapel is the same white as the dress of the honored girl.

The *chambelanes* are tuxed out like me and the *damas* are matched in their bright pink empire-waist gowns that run all the way down to the heels. Corsages on their wrists. I'm the only one wearing glasses. Pimply and fuzzy on the upper lip. We're all lined up behind the *quinceañera* and her beau, marching in procession to the altar where we fan out and take our places in the pews.

Everyone is looking at the priest as he gives his blessing to this fifteen-year-old who I know for a fact has been doing it with this white dude war vet in his Chevy Nova whenever they get the chance. My eyes, though, are on her cousin, who's kinda been hitting on me the whole time. At the *salón* where we practiced our procession the night before, she came to me and nobody else and asked me to help her carry the decorations in from her car. She looks a little like Natalie Wood in West Side Story, except her skin really is brown. A shade of brown that knocks me out. Later at the pot luck, she brought me a paper plate of mini-*flautas* and *frijoles*, for me, no one else but me, 'cause I was setting up the speakers for the deejay in the backyard. She smiled like Maria when she first sees Tony and asked me if it's okay if she got me a 7-Up 'cause they're all out of Coke. Usually, I can't stand 7-Up, but that night it was the elixir of the goddess.

At the Mass, I see her in the pew, her fine dress hiked way up her thigh. Her hair all done up with some kind of flower in it. She smiles when the *quince* receives her special Bible from the priest, then turns to me, to me alone, and extends the slightest, most imperceptible nod, as if she's saying yes to all the implausible fancies building up in my throat like a song. It's almost not even a nod, but because I notice it, I know it's meant for me.

We arrive at the *salón,* which is really VFW Post 8782. Everything decorated for the *baile.* Here they dance amid the draping streamers to the music of some cover band that has to know all the current hits in addition to the basic playlist of *rancheras* and *cumbias* that the adults expect. Fathers and uncles will get smashed and old women will tend to the little ones, while the older brats wander around trying to look down the *damas'* necklines. The *chambelanes* loosen their ties and some their cummerbunds to make room for the huge intake of beer and cake to come. I'm not drinking at all, partly because I'm not of legal age, but mostly because I'm keeping it together for the cousin. Soon as the lights dim and the slow number comes on, I'm taking her on the floor.

There it goes. *"Adoro."* Best make-out song ever. The couples swarm the dance floor and clutch each other tightly and I bee-line it to the cousin sitting there with her family. She turns and gives me that Natalie Wood smile like she's been expecting me the whole night.

Hey there, Mr. 7-Up. I was looking for you.

Yeah?

Can I ask you for a favor?

Anything.

Do you mind asking my sister to dance? She's a little bit shy but she really likes to dance.

Where is she?

She points out the sullen girl three chairs down with a strand of her hair in her mouth, drawing smiley faces in the drink rings on the table with her finger. She's about my age, but punier and darker-haired. I can tell she knows she's being talked about.

Okay, but I was thinking—

Puro gentleman. *Ándale*, before the song ends.

I nod a not so imperceptible nod and navigate through the tangle of metal folding chairs to ask her. She doesn't even look up, only shrugs and heads for the floor. I catch the glint of a metal brace on one of her legs. I notice that the shoe on the other foot is thicker by two inches. Polio, I'm guessing. She stands mute in the middle of all these couples swaying to the honey tempo of "*Adoro*," daring me to beat it out the door. I'm thinking all kinds of things I can't express, one of them being that I should, indeed, beat it out the door and catch a ride home before anyone sees me dancing with a cripple. But if Natalie Wood wants a favor that bad, okay. I walk up and take her sister's thin bony hand in mine and lay the other on her waist, and just like that, we're dancing. Or maybe just bobbing from side to side, but at least it's on the beat. I'm looking to see if Natalie Wood is watching, but she's not at her table. She's in the arms of this older guy with a major 'fro, a good dancer too, and he's got her real close and laughing. Now I know what the flirting was all about. This sister of hers, who won't even look at me. I smell the perfume on her, way overdone, but nice. She's chewing gum too, probably for her breath. Her small chest brushes once against the ruffles of my shirt, causing her eyes to flit timidly from blank space to blank space. She's dark like her sister, but not so dark I can't see her blush. I feel it in the warmth of her hand too, which is relaxing knuckle by knuckle into mine. I'm thinking this ain't so bad. I'm thinking she'd be prettier if she didn't have to be so tough, a hardass bitch in a bitch world. I'm thinking all kinds of things different from the ones I thought before, like am I the first one she's danced with tonight and does that make a difference, like how strange that this big shoe with the triple-sole is forcing us off the beat, and like how suddenly we land in that song between the song that touches on sadness and longing and the strange erotic charge of loneliness that only the unwanted feel.

"*Adoro*" segues into another slow ballad that keeps us swaying. I feel her body settle into mine a little more as my hand inches further along the small of her back. She's breathing into my shoulder. I'm not thinking anymore. I'm going to go home and not tell anyone about this ever, and I'm going to hate her sister and be grateful to her at the same time for the mercies tendered, and when I get my picture in the mail from the *quince* in my tuxedo, I'm going to remember that spot on the shoulder where the girl in the metal brace laid her breath. But now that the song is done, a more upbeat number is kicking in and I'm asking her with all the sincerity I can muster if she'll dance with me some more. She's already shambling to the table with a shake of her head, saying, You can't dance for shit.

THE SISTER

IN THE THICK DROWSE OF summer, that hypnotic Texas heat of mid-June, I take my mother's car without asking her, to drive by the house of the girl I have an excruciating crush on. I'd sat in my room listening over and over to the grinding wheeze of the air conditioner thinking about how I was gonna make it past summer without seeing her in the halls at school. I tried staring at her picture in the yearbook, but there's no grainy black-and-white of her anywhere in those pages. I had no choice but to see her. Just a glimpse to ease my pain. So here I go with the radio blasting Grand Funk for courage to the street where she lives.

I turn into her block and cruise slowly past a boy in a plain white tee-shirt idly pedaling his bike. He's got that look of benign disregard on his face that we all put on in public. Then I see the nondescript little bungalow where she lives. Compact, entirely sealed off from summer and horny sophomores, the blue curtains drawn hard against me. She has to be home. Where else is she going to be on a blistering late afternoon like today? She's in there contemplating the drone of her own air conditioner. Maybe if I circle around again, she'll defy all probability and come out in her cut-offs to water her lawn and wave at me like she's never done before. I turn off the radio and make a hard left and head for her street one more time. As soon as I round the corner, I see the boy lying in the middle of the street next to his bike. Just lying there. He was coasting the midafternoon thermals just seconds ago, and now there he sprawls right in front of my car. My mother's car. Which she will begin to miss right about now. I look around and wait for somebody to come to this boy, who looks like he's melted right into the asphalt. The front tire of his bike is spinning like a roulette wheel. I turn off the engine and get out to check on him. His eyes are open, he's breathing in short rapid gasps, but he seems to be caught in some kind of spell. There's a deep scrape on his forearm and little bits of grit from the road on his face. I say, Hey. I say, *Vato*, you okay? I say, What happened, *ese*? But he keeps staring straight up at that bleached-out sky. I see coming out from under him a small puddling of what appears to be motor oil, but I know it's not motor oil. I look all around again for somebody to see him, to claim him, to relieve me of this appalling fact of pain. But it's just him and me. I take his arm and raise him up a little bit to help him to the curb when I see this bloody tear in the back of his tee-shirt. I lift it up a bit until I can see his skin and there I see a long thick gash spitting out burbles of blood. I say, Man, this is not good. His eyeballs roll back into his skull like he wants to take a look at that gash too. And that's when all these people suddenly appear out of nowhere, yelling at me. Especially this one person who appears to be his older sister. She's yelling all kinds of curses in Spanish at me, grabbing and glaring at me like I brought this shit down on her brother. I tell her I found him this way and I think he got stabbed, but she's not hearing me. She's hysterical, she's in shock, she knows some bad shit's happened, and the best she can do right now is take it out on me. People hold her back and I want to leave, I want to get the hell away and go home, but nobody lets me. Some guy goes through my pockets, hoping to find a knife, I guess, and I get pissed when he pulls out my wallet. I snatch it back and yell at them to leave me the fuck alone. The sister screams, What did you do to my little bro! I yell back, BITCH, NOTHING! I yell it so loud in her face, I yell it with such naked ferocity that she stops crying and steps back a bit. Everyone riveted. The sun pile-driving us into the street.

Almost immediately, the cops and an ambulance arrive. The EMTs attend to the boy. I tell the cop about the cut along his back. Probably some fucker in a passing car slashed at him, I say. He says, Did you see it happen? I say, No. I say, I found him this way. Then the boy groans and I know he's going to be all right. The sister is still glaring knives at me, but the cop pulls me aside and tells me that she's only scared and confused and to let it go. That's when I realize that my own eyes have been locking murder on her too. I say yeah and get back in my mother's car and maneuver carefully, slowly past the bike and the blood puddle in the street, past the sister's unrelenting glare, past the other girl's house with the blue curtains and, through my hot tears, drive myself home. Such hate in my heart. Such hate.

FRED'S HERB

LA PLEVE MEANS THE PEOPLE. That much I know. We toss around the terms of our *pleve* in this niche in the desert like coin of the realm. *Ese* means hey. *La lisa* means the shirt. *Calcos* are shoes. *Ranfla* means bike, unless you own a car, in which case it means that too. *Rucas* and *vatos* are the chicks and dudes of our hood, and they all live in their separate *chantes*, or houses. To us little shits of twelve and thirteen, command over the jargon of our *cultura* means we got that much more cool in our mouths. Unbutton your *lisa* when you ride your *ranfla*, *vato!* And *wáchale!* Don't scuff my *calcos, ese!* We are taking English and dropping its chassis, adding some hot rims and sidewalls and detailing it with our own style.

There's a new word among us now finding favor in the vernacular. *Joto*. I don't know what it means exactly, but we call each other that all the time. *No mames, joto!* You're such a *joto!* Don't be a *joto* and lend me a *bola*. I know *bola* right away. A monetary unit equal to a dollar. Twenty *bolas* buys you a ticket to the concert, but you can still be a *joto* if some *vato* chooses to call you that. My *jefe*, that is, my dad, he doesn't like that term. Don't let them call you that, he says. Why not? 'Cause *es falta de respeto*. But lack of respect is way too common among us to make any difference. Consequently, I start calling my buddies *jotos* whenever I want to throw some localspeak around.

But now it's high school and somehow, most of that idiom has fallen away from our speech, like crumbs of stale bread. But not *joto*. We may inflect our Spanglish with Shakespeare and Twain and Anne Frank, but *joto* remains a vital pejorative on our lips. It's got some color and therms and a healthy dose of coarseness. When we wanna give somebody shit who deserves it, we say, *Qué pasó, joto*, I heard you were saying things behind my back. It's a word that exists among us, for us, which means it's never heard on TV or the radio or anywhere but on the streets and classrooms of the *pleve*.

But it's there in the classroom that I get to know Fred. He's a year ahead of me and one of the better actors in our drama club. Tall, thin and smiley and one of the few white kids in our school, Fred also happens to be the swishiest boy I've ever known. He can't help it. Just like he can't help but be the kindest sweetest kid in the group, he can't help but mince when he walks, squeal when he talks, cross his legs in the most effeminate way and swing his arms around with a flourish. There's nothing sans serif about him. He's like Jack Lemmon in Some Like It Hot, except in plaid shirt and jeans. But for all his sunshine grins he's got a side of burnt toast too. Sometimes, he sulks in a corner by himself, turning red as only a *gabacho* can, ravenously biting his nails as he pretends to read his Midsummer's monologue, and sometimes he snaps at people who ask him if he's okay. I'm FINE, he snarls, his bony shoulder wheeling around his taut freckled face.

This is usually when we let Fred work out his kinks in private. That broodiness is sometimes too much to take. But this day, I feel something for the guy. I dunno what it is. Something outside the vocabulary of my experience. I go to him and sit down and don't say a word 'cause I know he'll shred it in mid-air. I just watch him pick at a freckle on his wrist for a while. Then he says, I hate this monologue. I nod and ask which. Oberon's monologue about the stupid flower. He wants Puck to fetch it for him. It has a potion to make people fall in love in spite of themselves. But that's dumb. You can't make people like you.

It's a comedy, Fred.

I know, he drawls. He wipes his eye with the heel of his palm and sighs heavy as a dog then laughs ever so lightly to cancel it out. He looks at me at last and with a thin smile says, Wouldn't it be nice, though?

Did something happen?

Nothing I can't handle. Some days are just harder than others.

You need anything, Fred, you let me know.

His gaze settles back on his freckle and for a second, I see all his prior smiles tumble into each other, spiral down into some opacity only he has the map for, a place he huddles in for solace and balm. Then just as quick, he's back, throwing that chin of his in my face with a big smile as he takes up his Midsummer once again.

Well, since you put it that way, junior. Fetch me this flower. The herb I showed thee once.

And he laughs and I show him my middle bird and he laughs again louder. The flighty happy Fred is back and we're all happy for it.

Later in the day, as the bell rings us out of school, we head for our waiting buses. I see the usual row of matted-haired *vatos* leaning on the walls or crouched on the floor of the foyer where the halls converge. I know them by their super-flared bell-bottoms and unbuttoned *lisas* and their dirtheeled *calcos*, the same *rucos* who light up their unfiltered *frajos* in the smoking section of the school. I see them nod their heads and make hurting sounds at the goodness walking by, that is, the *hainas* shuffling past in their miniskirts. The girls just let their long hair shield them from the stares and catcalls and move on, and my heart sinks for them. Then I see Fred. He's walking through the foyer with his satchel, eyes ahead, aware of them, only too conscious, but he has to pass through this gauntlet, so he powers on, trying not to swish, but in his urgent need to get past them, he swishes even more, and his throat turns bright red, his hand impulsively bats at some evil cobra in his way, and his mouth tightens to a line as they begin their catcalls. *Joto. Oye, joto.* You're so cute. Be my girlfriend, *joto. Pinche joto maricón.*

Now I know what *joto* means. Now I understand its proper use. And I guess Fred knows it too. His tight-lipped half smile tells me so. *Joto.* I wanna tell these jackasses the harm they do. I wanna show them the scum smeared inside the shell of that word. But I can't. I've said it too. I said it this morning. I've said it for the last five years, the last five million years, since before I was born, since before Fred even knew what that word meant, since the day someone else came up with that word in another language, in every language, since the ancient word for faggot and *manflora* and nigger and kike and spic and *gringo salado.* It's a slang of its own disgrace, an idiom of idiots, conjugated by ignorance. As Fred thrusts the doors wide to the afternoon sun and goes who knows where, I realize how that word makes some days so much harder than others.

JESUS IN OUR MOUTHS

I WIN AN ESSAY CONTEST when I'm 17. It's the year of the Bicentennial, and it's about America and patriotism and God. Two other girls from my school are traveling with me to Brownwood, Texas, to present our essays before large appreciative audiences from all over the state.

It's a long drive to this place. We go in a rented van, the three of us and our teacher who is in the habit of saying Praise God all the time. In fact, she says it so often, we started saying it too.

We'll need to stop and get some gas.

Praise God.

The baloney sandwiches are good.

Praise God.

We'll be there before dark.

Praise the Lord.

That evening in Brownwood, we get a tour of the Douglas MacArthur Academy of Freedom and admire his corncob pipe. American flags everywhere. Then we go to a big ranch house where a huge buffet spread is laid out for us. There must be about thirty people there. And they say Praise God too. After we eat some more sandwiches and mashed potatoes, this man gets up and gives witness, that is, he tells us how he found Jesus and let him into his heart, and then we all stand in a wide circle, hold hands, close our eyes and pray. I hear my teacher leading the prayer, intent and passionate, then someone else's voice takes up where she leaves off, and so on. My eyes are clamped shut as I try hard to feel the rapture in the room, but I just can't get into it. I really need to pee.

I'm fairly certain it's a man holding my left hand because I can feel his big class ring digging into my pinkie, but nestled in my right is a smaller, softer hand. A girl's hand like a little bird with bird smoothness, warm and tentative. I don't know who she is, or what she looks like, but it doesn't matter. We're two hands randomly clasped together in this circle of faith. I'm not sure if all the overheated praying has anything to do with it, but I sense our pulses quickening. Amen, someone cries. I feel her press against my hand and I send that pressure back as softly as I can. I caress her knuckle with my thumb, slowly at first, imperceptibly, like I'm not even aware of it myself. Then I feel her fingernail drawing circles on the back of my hand. Amen, I hear again. Our palms now moist, fingers caress and lace and chafe against the urges inside. Through her hand I touch every intimate part of her as she whispers oh yes Lord yes Lord oh yes. This goes on for a while obliterating all the prayers in the room and when the last amen of many is uttered, we open our eyes and regard each other for the first time. She's a pretty Permian Basin girl with large penetrating blue eyes and straw-blonde hair. Pure West Texas loveliness. That's what I see. What she sees I can't say. But her neck breaks out in a rash all the way down to her chest.

While everyone goes for seconds at the buffet table, I go to the bathroom and then sneak outside to the large sloping backyard. I find a bench in an arbor and quietly sit in the dark and cry. I don't know why but the sobs just burble up like they've been waiting for this time. Then before I know it, the Permian Basin girl is sitting beside me, holding my hand again just as tightly as before, and she's crying too. I'm ashamed and I say so, but she won't let me say anything more. We just huddle in that arbor crying and then kiss like crazy fools for a while, digging our tongues deep into each other, finding Jesus in our mouths.

The next morning, we read our essays in this huge auditorium and I put everything I've got into mine. It's all about Love of God and Country and the righteousness of our Christian nation, but I'm feeling none of it. I don't want to pray and I don't want to tell America how great she is and I don't want to be 17 anymore. I want to get back in the van and go home. Not with Jesus in my heart but the ghost pressure of her hand in mine taking me there.

I get a letter from her a few weeks later, a sweet note saying hello and how much she'd like to see me if I come by town again, and how that night with me has made a difference she didn't expect. I can feel her Permian Basin heart in every word. But all over the letter, in almost every other sentence, she writes Praise God.

CISCO

MY DAD CAME HOME, PUSHED my homework aside and told me. We had some trouble at work. Cisco's not there no more.

With his knowing smirk, teen idol hair and blue-grey eyes that twinkle for the girls, Cisco is the coolest guy in our taco shop. There he is, slung over the juke box selecting "Nineteen Hundred and Eighty-Five" by Wings for the third time that day. Tall and slim with his puka bead necklace on a smooth, slightly sunken chest, an easy shuffling gait that can't be hurried, he's the picture of everything I want to be. I'm so into that natural cool, but the *señoras* at work find him irritating. They can't make him do what they want. Clean the trays, Letty tells him. Clean them yourself, he'll fire back with a laugh. He always tells me to ignore them. They like to boss people around 'cause it makes them feel important, he says. Sometimes when he makes Letty really sore, she goes to my dad, who sternly calls him into the kitchen—Francisco!—and Cisco without thinking twice, goes when he's summoned, composed and respectful. My dad admonishes him but gently, telling him to ease off on Letty, and Cisco dutifully nods. Always that invisible wink between them, though.

It's good you don't work the weekdays, my dad says. *Porque algo pasó. Algo muy mal.*

Even Letty has to confess that work is a lot more fun with him around. She tells me he's like a kid brother who is just too good-looking for his own good. She nags him all the time, but if you ask me, it's 'cause she's got a secret crush on him and he could care less. Cisco's got his eyes dead-set on the white chicks.

I marvel at his way with them. He's especially smooth with the blondes on their lunch break from the bank or the girls from the service department at the Western Auto. *Las viejas*, he calls them. *Las babys*. I watch him take an order at the counter when they come up. With his eyes lowered to his pad and pencil, he works that trilling accent to his advantage, all while he's smirking like he knows something they don't. It's how he lets the girls admire him undisturbed. Then he'll look up and pretend he doesn't know a certain word they just said and he'll lean in toward them, ask them to repeat it, and then they laugh together. When the orders are ready for pick-up, we call out the numbers on the tickets. Not Cisco. He calls out their names.

When the lunch rush is done and there's time to chow down on some *taquitos*, he likes to hang with me. He's captivated by my vocabulary. How do you know so many big words? They're not so big, I tell him, they just sound that way. He wants me to teach him. He says he'll show me how to pick up girls if I teach him a few words so he can sound more like he's from here. I ask him if he's ever been apprehended by the immigration agents. *Muchas veces*, he admits. Too many times. They just drive me to the bridge and drop me off, but next day, I'm back. He chuckles, then shows me all these little shreds of napkins in his wallet with names and phone numbers. Kristin. Vicky. Melanie. Gina Lee. Rachel. What's the deal with the white girls, I ask him. I like how they are so free, he says. These *gabachas* don't care. They got . . . how do you say *confianza*? Confidence, I tell him. He nods and smiles as he sounds the word out. One of these *babys*, he says, is going to be my confidence. I'm going to marry her and become semi-*gabacho* like you. Which honestly makes no sense to me, since I want to be like him.

Cisco?

Yes, Dad says. He tells me the INS raided the place. Just as they were opening, three men in uniform and one in a suit walked in the employee door and started yelling. Conchita, who works in the kitchen, hid under the metal prep table between two large pots, which is something 'cause she's over sixty and not as spry as the others. They found her first. Then they looked in the walk-in freezer and there behind the shelves, they found Cisco. When he made a joke about the length some people go to get free tacos, they slammed him to the floor and cuffed him. He bled from his nose all over his beautiful shirt. The agents made everyone, even my dad, show their proof of citizenship and work visas. They cited Mr. Alarcon for hiring illegal aliens and said they were going to visit the other shops in the franchise. It was an ugly scene, Dad said, played out right in front of the customers, who stood there at the counter watching the whole thing, and how Letty and the others felt ashamed and scared for Cisco and Conchita, but went ahead taking orders for tacos with the tears settling in the creases of their smiles.

Some weeks later at work, I ask Mr. Alarcon if he's heard any news 'cause nobody seems to be talking about it. He says Conchita was deported to Juárez and won't be coming back. As for Cisco, they decided to make an example of him for all his previous violations. He's in La Tuna, serving a long sentence in that hellhole of a prison, he says. That boy's not going to make it in there. Is there anything we can do? Can we help him? The manager shakes his head and says we can't get involved anymore. We're in enough trouble as it is. But he adds that Cisco told him that he had at home a whole wad of napkins with the phone numbers of friends who would bail him out in no time. He was confident of that.

Somehow, I don't think that happened.

DEMON

EVERY CORNER OF THE WORLD has its changeling, and Demon broods in ours. With his solemn Mayan face sloping back to a scalp nicked with the hieroglyphs of old corrections, his eyes crossed and bloodshot, he is the oldest of our tribe, the smallest, and the least capable of grasping the long straws of his simple life.

When my parents move us to a house just a half mile from the Rio Grande, it doesn't take long for us to meet the other kids in the area. Striking friendships we think will last forever, we play street football, ride our banana-seat bikes up and down the dried irrigation ditches, play hide-and-go-seek till nightfall and liven up our summers with sno-cones and monkeyshines. Somehow, Demon is a part of all that. He just shows up one night and sits down with us while we tell ghost stories. He doesn't say a word, just sits on our porch and nods like a monk every now and then. I see his dirty scabbed elbows and his hands, small and calloused as a rancher's, and wonder what he's been through. When my mom calls us in, he abruptly jumps to his feet and shuffles off.

Who's he, I ask Kino, one of our newfound *camaradas*.

That's Demon.

Demon?

A toda madre. He's cool.

What's his real name?

Kino thinks for a second. I dunno.

Where does he live?

Somewhere over there, I think.

For a few days, nobody sees him around. We don't really miss him, but we wonder about him anyway. Then he'll turn up like he was always there. I'll spot him from the back seat of the car trudging along Alameda Street in a pair of stiff jeans too big for him. There goes Demon, I say to Mom and Dad. *Pobrecito*, my mom says back.

We all kinda know something's not right with Demon but nobody mentions it. We treat him like one of the team, except when we wanna play Dare. We dare him to do the riskiest shit 'cause we know he'll always comply. He'll jump into Mr. Martinez's yard to steal some peaches from his tree for us. He'll throw water balloons at the Border Patrol vans for us. He'll run to the girls from down the street to ask them if they'll hike their dresses up for us. He'll get into some ugly fights too. He takes on kids bigger than him and even when he's losing, he doesn't quit. He's fearless. But he also does the things that we'd never dare anybody. Like suck enamel spray off a sock for hours at a time. I catch him once crouched in a culvert, rattling that ball bearing in a can of semi-gloss white. When I ask what he's doing, he shrugs and does that thing with his mouth that he thinks is a smile and shoots some spray into a tube sock. Then he turns away and inhales it with an audible hiss. I see him teeter on his haunches for a long minute, his head bobbing on his shoulders like it's about to come off, and I guess that's one of the reasons people call him Demon.

He doesn't seem to go to school 'cause we don't see him in any of our classes. And by the time we get to high school, we don't see much of each other, either. We outgrow our Demon days. Meanwhile, he becomes a solitary urchin roaming the hood with a rag and pail, asking people if they want their car washed. Later on, he'll give up the pail and just ask people for change.

But I'm not thinking about that. I'm three-quarters through my freshman year at Riverside High and I've been seeing this girl. She lives far out in the Ysleta school district and I have to hop a bus to see her. We talk a little on her porch with the light out and then spend the next hour or so kissing and feeling each other up. We get to the point where we can't go any further without doing something stupid and then we say goodnight. I walk back to the bus stop and ride the long dissatisfaction home.

The bus stops near Midnight and Alameda and I get off and start walking down my street. There's no moon in sight and the trees throw dense shadows in my path. I hear the chink-chink of a keychain, someone walking behind me, and I think maybe some *vatos* in their gang are looking to jump me. I quicken my pace. Then I hear my name called in a dull syrupy voice I haven't heard in years. I slow down to let Demon catch up. I can't see his face, but I know it's him. He's wearing his jacket zipped up and the same stiff pair of old jeans bunched up at the ankles.

Hey, Demon.

¿Cómo te va, güey?

I'm nervous around him for no reason but I tell him I'm fine and ask him where he's been.

Por aquí, por allá.

Yeah, I've been around too. I just came from my girlfriend's house.

¿O sí?

He asks that in such an oblique way, like he wants to know more, like maybe he doesn't know what a girlfriend is. Maybe he just wants to make conversation. I tell him I almost did it with this girl. I tell him she's crazy beautiful and we're all hot and heavy for each other, but I don't know if it'll work out because she lives so far.

¿Muy lejos?

All the way to Ysleta, I tell him. He stops and looks in the direction that I'm pointing, then he says, That ain't far, *güey.*

It is far, Demon.

Almost every week I walk that. To see my *tía.*

Your aunt lives out there?

No. She's dead. She's buried in Socorro.

I'm sorry, *ese*.

He explains to me that he's not. He explains that his mother didn't want him and it was his aunt that raised him from a baby, but she didn't take care of him like she was supposed to. He had some checks coming every month from the government and *tía* kept all the money. Now she's gone too and all he has is her grave to visit.

Pues, why do you go?

He shrugs and holds his hand to his chest like his heart's about to leap out. I think of all the things we made him do, all the dares he undertook to be one of us, and how none of it made a difference anyway. 'Cause look where we are now. He comes back around to the subject of my girlfriend and remarks that it's not the distance I'm afraid of. It's her.

What do you mean?

You're scared you might do it with her, *güey*. And then you'll have a baby and who's going to take care of that shit, right? *¿Verdad?*

I'm about to tell him he's wrong, that there's a lot of guys out there who married really young and started families and they still get to follow their dreams, even if their dreams are small-time and probably hamstrung by family concerns, but he stops and mutters hey in that thick sleepy voice and unzips his jacket a little as he gestures me toward him.

With some apprehension, I look in the crook of his jacket and I think I see something moving, but it's too dark to see what. I'm afraid it might be some ugly thing he's saved up just for me. But then he opens his jacket wider and shows me a small bird, a sparrow nestled in his chest. It seems so still and unreal but when I reach my hand in, it flutters weakly against his shirt. Where'd you get it?

I found it. Its wing is broke. A cat almost got it.

What are you gonna do with it?

He tells me he's going to take care of it till it heals and then he's going to let it go at his aunt's gravesite. I tell him it's a real decent thing to do and that I hope it heals quick.

He nods more times than he should and then starts veering off to wherever his house is. Wherever forgotten changelings go. But there's still something I have to know.

Demon, what's your real name?

He stops in the middle of the dark street and turns around. He waits a while like he can't believe I asked that question. I hear the bird against his chest.

You already know it, he says.

I can't see his face, just the outline of that large tapered head, but I think he's doing that thing with his mouth that he thinks is a smile. Chink-chink goes his keychain.

MEXICAN APOLOGY

MEXICANS DON'T KNOW HOW TO say sorry. For one thing, we don't have the words in Spanish for it. *Lo siento* is what comes out. But that means I feel it. I know what you're feeling. I empathize. A true apology, though, that's hard to phrase in the Mexican mouth.

Which is strange. Because sorry is what we're all about. In our backyard having a glass of iced tea without the ice, I'm looking over the fence at the skinny brown kids riding their bikes to the bazaar being held in the church parking lot. Like I used to do before my bike got stolen. The makeshift booths are already glowing with strands of tiny blinking lights. There's a DJ spinning discs for the *gente* who are throwing their dimes into cups for a chance at the Pink Panther plush toy. From where I stand, I see the sun's last oblique rays setting on the *lotería* booth, where already someone in a flat nasal voice is calling out *¡La Sirena! ¡La Sirena!* over the P.A. For sure, mermaids in the middle of the desert might be common as priests, like the one strolling among the throngs, nodding this way and that, smiling at everyone and placing the cup of his hand on the backs of the little ones' heads.

All this is foreign to me now. All this is something I no longer want any part of. Some ugliness poisoned it for me years ago and none of it holds any charm in my heart this time.

My father comes out in his slippers, his bottle of Tecate foaming at the mouth. He holds it like a club and looks around for something to not talk about. He was born with an angry face, so even when he's pensive, he looks like he's about to slap someone across the cheek with a brick. He stands in his shorts and cotton shirt looking at the crowds milling through the bazaar, then takes a slug of his beer. The bottleneck is all knuckles when he drinks. Finally, he nods to me. I nod back. Taking this as a sign that we could be exchanging more than nods pretty soon, I turn my back and look over the other fence at the scrappy tufts of grass in our front yard. The words *not now* are riding the carousel in my head. *Not now, not now, not now.*

I can feel him shuffling closer, this man who shares his name with me, as the voice over the P.A. calls out another card. *¡La Escalera!* The ladder. Our Mexican bingo doesn't mind mixing the mundane with the archetypal. It's all the same to us, if we really think about it. All part of this hard life where the days pass like kidney stones and the nights are remembered for the sobbing and the cursing and the fists through the walls. He stops behind me where I can't see what he's looking at, but I know his eyes land on everything but me. I'm this blind spot he's never figured out how to talk to, though I think he's going to try now.

A couple more shuffles and he's right beside me, resting his arms on the chest-high fence next to mine. We're both looking straight ahead at the slow parade of cars passing us on their way to the bazaar. The greasy smell of *gorditas* frying on the skillet lends a little grace to the moment, but only a little. We're both tense as fuck standing in the waning light of a sun sick and tired of our bullshit.

I make out his profile against the wall of our *casita*. He's breathing into his huge hands like they're a pair of bellows. I used to believe I was another man's son, I used to think he took me as his when he married my mother, I used to think that for no other reason than I wanted to. After all, what the hell do we have in common except a roof and a name? I see his drawn brooding features now and no question about it, he's my *jefito* and I'm his son. I was born with the same angry face. The voice in the P.A. announces the next card. *¡El Borracho!*

I'm thinking of all the things I need to tell him 'cause finally I'm big enough to take him on. I figure it will make my shit more justifiable if I turn into him for just this teenager moment. Let him see that angry face on me. What will you think of that, dear ol' Pop? But then I wonder, what if this angry face is all he's ever seen? What if it's me who turned him this way? I wasn't all that great a kid to raise, was I? I had my ugly moments too. I'm trapped in a thousand recriminations while behind us under the twinkling lights, families are placing their raw pinto beans on their *lotería* boards.

Amid the din of the bazaar, with all the children laughing and the mothers calling and the fathers throwing *gritos* in the air, I hear him say two words. Not the words I expect. But the words of a Mexican beaten down and tethered to the sins of fatherhood.

Era cabrón.

The words rise from his knuckles. Words that translate into *I was a shit. I was not myself. I was something I won't be from now on. I crapped all over your life, even when I meant well, and I know it. I won't be that again. I'm your father. And today your father is a changed man.* All in two words. They are as close to saying I'm sorry as anything in the lexicon of our culture. But it's the way his eyes skirt mine that tell me the staves of his heart are bursting with remorse, black and mean. I don't know if I look at him, but I think I do. I think

I nod again and say, It's okay, Dad. Something in me wishes I didn't mean it, but I do. 'Cause my own staves are cracking too.

He looks around again for something to moor him, but nothing avails itself, so he leaves the beer on the fence and shuffles back inside. I stand there watching the cooling air scatter the cottonwood seeds across this tired old town. My eyes go to the bottle and I see that he's only taken the one swig. Without even thinking about it, I take it by the neck and down one too, right from the same mouth.

¡El Corazón! cries the P.A.

THE RUNNER

BLUR IS WHAT HE IS. A blur of desperate motion. Fleshed with some kind of unknowable need. I'm in my eighteenth year, feeling the press of graduation in my chest, but this minute I am calm. Eating my breakfast. I feel his blur. The slap of a shoe padding across our porch gets me to the door. My first impulse is to see what's missing from our yard. When I'm satisfied nothing is taken, I turn to him already forty . . . fifty . . . a hundred feet away tearing at a full sprint. He's young, younger than me, hair so short the hieroglyphs in his scalp glisten. Wearing clothes his mother might have bought him at the K-Mart. A light plaid cotton shirt unbuttoned, flaring behind him like wings; jeans with the hems soiled and frayed, the tongue end of his long belt slapping against him with each stride; shoes foul with tramping through mud and standing water. He's dark and his hair is dark and he's getting smaller now, disappearing behind parked cars, reappearing as an even smaller runner on their other side. His shadow blurred to nothing. *Mira como va corriendo*, my mom says. It must be a *mojadito*. But he's nothing like the crossers we're accustomed to seeing. For one thing, they never run. They walk as if they belong. Like the air is full of trip-wires. Besides, there's no one chasing this guy. No Border Patrol van. No gangs. And ahead of him, nothing he's trying to catch up to. It's just him running like the demons are on him. His sins swarming over him. Some infernal blood driving him out of or into a purgatory he dreads or yearns for. I think he wants to sprint himself out of this turgid life, race out of his skin and his name and his past and his destiny till his breath is all that defines him, those deep pants for air counseling him, urging him on; but before I dismiss the thought, before I realize how stupid I am to project on him my terrors, the dark bedeviled blur runs swiftly into the vanishing point and becomes it.

LA MARISCAL

WE SHOOT OUR MORTARBOARDS HIGH up in the air, pose for the Instamatics with our parents, bounce around some parties in the area and now it's time for whores. 'Cause we're eighteen, legal and free, our lives fully ours to blow, and yeah, some beer and *mota* for the jubilation, spinning the world with the flat of our hands, making the day bum-rush itself into night, four maniacs hanging out of our cars, waving and screaming and cheering like guerrillas at the end of a war. We stop at my house for some of Mom's *caldo de pollo* to steady the floor, give us pause. My mom pours us each a steaming bowl of laughter with some of that Mexican Coke and, bless her gracious heart, looks past our inebriation. We're not that drunk anyway; we just act like that to spur the giddiness on. While we slurp our *caldo* we talk about the school year, the good times and the shitty, the pretty girls we'll never see again, the damn bullies we'll never have to dodge, the courses we'll have nightmares about no more. My mom is right there, beaming through it all, but when she leaves, one of us says, Let's go. Go where? You know where. *Vato*, you mean *Juaritos*? I mean, *La Mariscal*. What for? You know what for. You serious? Serious as fuck. I don't know. C'mon, everybody goes, it's a rite of passage. You guys wanna? I will if you will. I will if *you* will. All these wills being passed around the table, not a single won't. So I tell Mom, we're driving over to Juárez. She says, Are you sure? We'll be okay. Be careful, *mijo*. We'll be all right. We're fucking heroes tonight, Mom, I wanna say. We own this night.

We stop at the drug store, pick up a packet of rubbers and pile back into the car. We try one on to see how they fit and it's the funniest shit we've ever seen. It don't work if it ain't hard. The drive over the Bridge of the Americas is swift and easy, no hassle, no waiting, and soon, we're in the bar district near where we wanna go. We pay an attendant ten bucks to park our car and keep it safe for us, and we head into the first club. The lights are strobing to the pounding disco beat. The drinks are cheap, sweet and strong. The bartenders are short and dark and they don't smile. We overtip but they don't seem impressed. Disgusted, in fact. But they swipe the Lincolns off the bar just the same. The girls sitting in a booth at the back, talking Spanish and smoking like sailors, they're mighty cute, their short skirts showing off their sturdy legs. They don't want shit to do with us, though. One of us tries to buy them some frou-frou drinks, but they shift their bodies away and draw their hair over their faces, while one of them sneers, *No te metas donde no te llaman, pinche gringo*. Hey, we say, we ain't no *gringos*. We're Mexicans like you! Without missing a beat, the bartender takes our drinks off the bar and says, *Buenas noches, señores*. Fuck you all, we cry and stagger out full of the bluster of the moment into the searing Juárez night. *Gringos*. Where do they get off? *¡Somos como ustedes!* All of you and us, we're the same people! Just 'cause we're born over there, that don't mean shit! Cars grind along the narrow streets, every other one a crummy taxi jammed with more besotted graduates. We look at each other and one of us says, Time for *La Mariscal*. Now? Now. Are you sure? Why not? Are we ready? We got rubbers, don't we? There's a man in a black cowboy hat holding a *guitarrón* standing outside a bar and I ask him for directions to *La Calle Mariscal. Por allá*. That way? Yes. That way. So that way *nos vamos*.

We turn a corner into a wide lane closed off to traffic and walk along the broken sidewalk toward the clubs and storefronts. The streetlights are burned out and it's hard to see. We are getting pumped up for this. Or maybe we think we are. We're tittering like eighth graders on a field trip, making jokes and flashing the condoms to passing drunks. A man in a *guayabera* with his hair slicked back sits outside a door smoking Virginia Slims and through the doorway we see some women talking. We ask, *¿Cuánto por la hora?* But he doesn't answer. Maybe he thinks we don't mean it, and maybe he's right. We pass another stoop with an immense woman in the tightest short dress I've ever seen and again we ask how much? Without looking at any of us, she says in her broken English, how much you want, and grabs her own monstrous tit. We crack up like it's the punch line to some inside joke and back away, but already I feel my teeth chattering. At the next door, there is no door, but a red dirty curtain on a curtain rod. A man in a bow tie and dinner jacket comes out, a baseball bat in his right hand, and he's no dilly-dally. You want girls, *muchachos*, I got girls here, come, I got many girls for you. He keeps waving us over, the bat hid behind his leg, and his grin looks more like a grimace. We're already mumbling no thank you, no thank you, but the man feels no sinew in our words. He takes one of us by the arm, it could be me, it could be all of us at once, and pulls us toward the greasy curtain. With a magician's flourish, he draws it back to show us a garishly lit room with a large poster of Elvis, the words "Love Me Tender" inscribed at the bottom. Then a bed presents itself to us and dancing on it like a stripper is a naked young girl, she might be twelve, she might be our kid sister, and she looks tired and high and probably fucked into a stupor. The man says, Very clean, *muchachos*, she do anything for you, anything. We're shaking our heads, feeling like it's time to go home, but also feeling, to our disbelief, to our dismay, to our bitter shame, a little hard. I tell the man, We're just looking, thank you. The man yanks the curtain shut, and says, *Cabrones gringos turistas*. Always just looking, *¿verdad? Pues, que se vayan a la chingada, pinches babosos.* Don't call us that, we're solid *Mexicanos*, one of us protests. The man raises the bat like he's looking for an inside slider and hisses through his gold teeth, your *padres* are *Mexicanos*, but you, you are nothing but *gringos* to me! *¡Lárgense!*

For a full hour, we wander around trying to figure out where we left the car. By the time we find it and pay the attendant, one of us has thrown up my mom's *caldo de pollo* and another has decided to marry his girlfriend instead of trooping off to college. We count our measly dollars and somberly drive over the river back to where we're heroes. Only we're no heroes and we never owned the night. The night, in fact, owned us. She's the true whore slipping off our assumptions like a pair of dirty shorts and dancing on the condoms of our sweet American life for whatever it's worth.

TUMBLE-DOWN

I'M A YEAR INTO COLLEGE, home for the summer. One of those
blistering late afternoons that turn us into stupefied lizards.
The Brady Bunch is already into daytime reruns. I'm wondering what guys see in Marcia Brady. Her vaunted purity,
her flyaway hair, maybe the idea of a sanctified sister keeping
all the horny boys in check. Which I tell myself is not me. By
chance, I glance out the window at the girl standing on the
corner like she's waiting for Rhett Butler. Her black hair and
umber skin stand out against the frilly white dress, high heels
and white ankle socks and, oh yes, a white parasol trimmed
with lace. She's looking like she's missed the last train to the
ball. I step outside, and when she smiles at me, I recognize
her. We were in fifth grade together, we went to the same
high school, we have each other's names on the burnt flat
of our tongues. Because I want to help, I offer her a ride.
She needs to go to this church. We go to this church. There's
some kind of wedding going on. I see the limo parked out
front, decked with white streamers and white balloons. I wait
in the car while she goes in. She's gone less than two minutes, then she comes back. He's in there, all right. We'll wait
for this wedding to be done, then she'll see him. She tries to
make small talk about how much she loves going with him to
Elephant Butte Dam. She laughs about how as a little girl,
she thought there were elephants in Elephant Butte Dam
but now that she knows there aren't, she's so . . . It is such
. . . She can't finish what she says. She's gnawing at her fake
nails. Her dress is drawn up to her thighs. I feel myself getting

hard. All of a sudden, we're making out. I don't know how it happens, but there we are, kissing and feeling each other up. Her skin is so brown it's almost black. I feel her up right in the middle of this blazing hot church parking lot, this girl I've known since the fifth grade, writhing and arching her body back so far, she almost lands in the back seat, and she cries out the name of this other guy, but I don't care because my mind is flashing for some reason on Marcia Brady. Who is judging me. Brushing her hair and judging me. Goodbye, Marcia Brady. You don't know this like I know this. This is ours, this is how we rip through our bliss. This is how. Then she starts to cry. Not Marcia but the girl. Grinds out these hard, disconsolate sobs like lug nuts are caught in her throat. Like she's coughing blood kind of sobs. It scares the fuck out of me. I think I have a crazy girl in my dad's car and I wonder about that white dress and parasol. I wonder about that guy in the church. I wonder why I stepped outside to see her in the first place. I should ask her if she's okay, but I'm shaking so hard I can hardly form the words. The people begin streaming out of the church and I have to drive away. She laughs and mutters his name again and finishes off her own palindrome with another laugh, then tells me to take her to this house, but she doesn't know where it is. So I drive around these strange neighborhoods I've never been to while she carefully scans houses for something familiar, for some sign that this is the place she wants. Finally, she tells me to stop in front of this tumble-down old house with exposed adobe bricks and bed-sheets for curtains. The house is set far back from the street, the front yard bristling with weeds and dog shit. She kisses me nowhere near my mouth and says she'll be right back. I watch her walk up the crumbling walkway to the front screen door and peer in for a second. Then she slips in. She doesn't even look back. I sit with her smell in the car. I wait, I wait for her, I wait for her till night falls, but she doesn't come out.

A WALL BETWEEN

THERE ARE MORE THAN FOUR walls in our kitchen. When I'm at the table and my brother walks in, another one shoots right up between us. It's invisible to my family but not to me, and surely not to him, but neither of us mentions it. He steps in to get some *leche* from the fridge while I sink my head into the *El Paso Times* like it's all in fine print without either of us saying boo, and he don't even look my way. That's how the wall works. We can be gabbing with my mom or my sister about anything under the western sun and it don't matter; my bro and me don't see or speak a word in any language to each other ever, unless silence is a language, and I'm beginning to think it is. We've applied a lot of it in the last couple years. Ever since that night. Which is another thing we don't talk about.

That wall follows us all over the house. We course past each other without any reaction, except for that subtle look that passes over our faces sometimes, like something died and we forgot to take it out. What's stinking up the works is all that bad blood between us. *What bad blood. What fucking night. I didn't say anything.*

One early evening, he's watching TV in his gym clothes, 'cause my brother is now a badass football player for our school. I can't believe how tall and hulking he's grown. Muscles like those my dad had wished for me. Of course, I don't give him more than a quick skimming glance 'cause that would piss off the wall, so I stand nearby focused on the TV show, which I don't even want to watch, and he's trying to be all cool and stretches his legs out to make himself seem more unperturbed by this skinny asshole home from college messing up his prime-time viewing enjoyment, but the wall pushes his legs back up against the couch and five seconds later, he's stalking off to his room where those other walls can seal him off from my view.

This wall's been growing thicker between my *carnal* and me for almost eight years now. It's so old that we take it for granted. Early on, we were thankful for it. It kept us from yelling mean shit and ripping each other's faces off, and later spared us the embarrassment and the pain of having to admit that one of us, or maybe both of us, were wrong. The worst could easily have been said many times, if it weren't for that wall, but then it might have crumbled to nothing if we'd said it anyway. Now it seems like, by keeping us from each other, that wall is validating its own separate existence. A weird consequence of abiding by its rules is that when my brother comes by, it's not only him I cancel out, but me. I'm disallowing parts of myself which I desperately need him to see. *Who's sorry now. What night. What pinche wall.*

My mom, though, is a walking votive candle. She's been praying for this wall to go away for years, though she's never really mentioned it either. Nobody has. That's how families are. We just wait for shit to right itself when it's time and if it doesn't, we give it more time. But the longer it takes, the harder it is to look even once in the direction of my own damn brother. The handsomest of us. The freest. The *carnal* walked to school with me and played Star Trek on the swing set out back in that old house where our purer, simpler childhood got left behind.

Just half a mile down the road from our house is another wall. This one is real. They put it up after I left for college when the government freaked out about all these people crossing the river at will. They laid down a big six-lane border freeway alongside of it, too, just to drive the point home. I've heard that people scale it, dig under it, find every possible way through it; it's been the subject of international condemnation and political debate, and yet the wall's still there. Just like ours. My mom tells me, though, that since I moved away to make my life somewhere else, my brother has begun to ask about me every now and then. She says he's proud of me and my accomplishments. This startling communiqué from the other side is hard to believe, given our longstanding *mierda*, but maybe it's his way of digging under the wall, his way of chipping at the wall's need for grudges and rancor between brothers.

Maybe that's why something is different today. My mom is flipping the *huevos estrellados*, causing them to spit and gurgle on the pan. I'm rinsing my plate over the sink and my dad is already lacing his breakfast with salt and green *chile*. Lurching in from his shower, still looking sleepy, my brother thrusts his face through the neckhole of his tee-shirt, his eyes consciously directed at the pan.

¿Que pasó, Mom?

Un caro que no pitó, she says with a laugh. She's always ready with the gag, like it makes any difference to the wall. *¿Quieres unos huevitos, mijo?* I got them fryin' right here for you.

I could eat. He turns to my dad and says, Morning, Dad.

Buenos días, mijo. How did you sleep?

My brother takes his time replying 'cause he wants to. He's become more deliberate these days. I slept okay, he says.

Sit down, Mom says.

Although my back is to him, I know he's looking at the chair where I've been sitting. I can feel the wall trying to figure out how long I'm gonna be around, I can feel it thinking that maybe it's better if my bro takes his breakfast in his room. I should shut the tap off and get going. Instead, I decide to wash the rest of the dishes in the sink. Why not, since I'm not really here anyway? Neither is he, for that matter.

My brother sidles around the table in our cramped little kitchen to the chair opposite the one I had breakfast in and plants himself there. Already, his morning looks shot. I glance over my shoulder and see his strong hands rubbing themselves into fists. He tries not to show it, but his jaw is tight, his eyes darkening with the grievances of the young boy who still haunts him, who craves to be understood but can't find the words, or maybe he has, maybe he always had the words, but they're carved into the wall where only he can see them, like a secret testimonial, scrawled on that fucking wall where they remain unspoken and unseen by us.

But it's my wall too. And on it are projected all the memories, good and bad, that we have shared, all the intimacies of childhood, the games, the laughter, the shit, the agonies of adolescence that brutalize us well past our teens, as well as my own personal family grievances and stories, in which I sought to grow myself away from them and failed them, but failed him more. I'm not washing dishes now. My hands are wrung around the kitchen towel so tight, the brown in my fingers is red, and I can't look at anything but the dead space between us. Even my parents are aware of the tautness; they've fallen silent, the spit of grease in the pan almost hissing, *What bad blood? What lost time?*

Someone's gonna say something. Someone's gonna lose his shit. I can feel it. It might be him. Or me. Or the wall might shove both of us out of this tiny house and into that bigger room called life where bitterness will work us over as it pleases.

We're held like this for a tense moment, then my dad reaches over for the carton of *leche* on the table, and our uneasy eyes track it as he proceeds to open it, like he always does, from the wrong side, peeling off the adhesive that binds the flaps together. We watch him awkwardly pouring the milk into his glass and we can't resist smirking at each other *through* the wall. If we lock eyes another second, if we allow ourselves a shared chuckle at this irrepressible quirk of our good father, if someone says anything at all in any tongue but silence, that wall is gone.

EL SEGUNDO

I'M AT THE WHEEL WHILE my mother and I tour the sun-seared
streets of El Segundo in her car, doing some drive-by ret-
rospection. I don't know why we need this at our age, but
we do. She points out that tenement apartment on old Paisano Street where she, my dad and her mother, my Mamá
Concha, all lived together. The facade is different, renovated with bright red fake brick, and the front yard is fenced
in now, but it's still the same old ratty place. We lived here
till I was five. Although I have little recall of anything that
came to pass within, the outer walkway and staircase where
we played bristle with sunlit idylls of childhood. My *carnalito* Gordo playing with his blocks, my near fall from the top
landing, the churning eighteen-wheelers barreling past like
buffalo on the move. I see myself rolling on my tricycle over
the uneven planks of the second-floor landing. I see, sometime before his death, Ernesto in my mom's arms as she tries
to nurse him in the doorway while my dad showers before he
goes off to his dishwasher job. I see Dad again through the
bars of the railing getting out of that used '58 T-Bird with the
gill slits on the side, smiling up at me and gesturing with those
powerful arms that he proudly shows off in that shirt with the
rolled-up sleeves, his hair slicked up and back in a bouffant
that merges Elvis with Cuco Sánchez. He races up the stairs
three steps at a time in those billowing pants and hoists me up
like a barbell with one hand and laughs the way he no longer
does. And there's old Candelaria next door, known to us as
Cande, *morena* like an *india*, shrunken down to her essence,

all smiles and wrinkles, taking me in her arms and letting me play with her earlobe. I can't remember how it was inside, but I peer with my infant eyes through the window and see myself in a dark room, supine in a crib, the smell of stale milk on me, turning my head toward this blue flicker, where I see with fear and fascination on the screen of Mamá Concha's TV this man with a scar on his forehead and bolts on his neck coming toward me in this elegant stagger. In my imagination, he's real, a tall, pale man who speaks halting English and watches over my sleep.

This was where you almost died, says Mom.

You mean, in that fall?

No, your father caught you before you fell. I mean the time you drank all that turpentine.

When Dad was painting the living room.

And he fell asleep and you drank it down like it was *leche*. He ran with you in his arms all the way to Hotel Dieu Hospital. The doctors pumped your stomach and saved you. *Estabas azul.*

I picture him sprinting through traffic, weaving in and around people in his sweaty shirt all the way up to Hotel Dieu at the base of the mountain, chasing down the last meager breaths in a body gone blue. Mom's told that story so often, with new details thrown in each time, that it seems more like a silent movie than something true now. Everything about this place seems unreal to me.

We pass the fire station where she used to take me as a toddler to stand on the sideboards of the gleaming red fire truck. I've seen some old Kodak snapshots with me and these hearty men in their suspenders posing atop the truck.

There's the old *mercado* where she used to get her groceries, which meant whatever she could cook on that old twin-burner hot plate. And there are the various low-end department stores where she shopped for our clothes, the pawn shops and outdoor market stalls where the lowest-income *gente* of both sides of the *río* come to pick through garments and shoes and cheap jewelry. Then turning off the main drag, we catch sight of the men with the dusty red flags standing in the street cajoling us into their parking lots. We must be near the footbridge to Juárez. In fact, I see the wall. We're a scant five blocks from the Franklin Canal and the dry riverbed border with Mexico.

Another turn and we're in the oldest, poorest section of El Paso, where people still live in those tiny one-story block houses with the chipped paint and exposed adobe. I see old ladies walking arm in arm with their long hair braided down their backs like steel cables. Children standing at the gate of their house, barefoot, in their soiled bibs and Dallas Cowboy tee-shirts, age-old resentments set deep in their black eyes. A few wiry homeboys in their wife-beaters and khakis hanging out at a corner park, sentries for the two girls frolicking on the swings and seesaw. It was once a kill zone of gang warfare, the toughest ward in the west, a place where stabbings and beatings were so routine, they weren't even making the news. Today the edge is off these raw-boned streets. I see a young Anglo couple standing at a street corner querying their cell phones for directions.

Now a large mural on the walls of the Sacred Heart Tortillería looms before us and we stop to take note of the various figures depicted. Pancho Villa sitting at a table with an order of Chico's Tacos. The beloved Father Rahm on his bicycle, a giant flaming heart suspended over him. A pair of border crossers wading across *el Río*, their path blazed by the flashlight held in the capable hands of *La Virgen de Guadalupe*. Even one of the alligators from San Jacinto Plaza stands guard at the base of Mexican Jesus on the cross. It's the sentimental history of our city with all our icons and heroes crowded into a single canvas of pale sky and grey earth with the mountain pinned against the background. Unreal as memory. Soon we coast past the red brick structure of Sacred Heart

Catholic Church and my mom tells me she came there a few times when we were little. Once, she says, after Ernesto died of pneumonia, and again when she came in desperation to make a plea. She told the presiding Father Gafford that my brothers and sister and I were starving and that she had no money for milk. She thought he'd pray for us, but instead, he took some dollars from his own pocket and handed them to her. He gave her money every week until my parents could stand on their own earnings. It was their secret. He was a very decent man who asked nothing in return, she says and falls silent as the memory of her need and his generosity penetrates some deeper layer of her being. Her eyes track the old church as it slips behind us in our motion forward. Then out of nowhere she bursts into sobs, untethered sobs from down in her soul, covers her face and collapses into the console between us, her whole body caught in this belated, unfinished grief. I'm shocked by the violence of her weeping. She can't even speak. The sobs rattle inside her like stones. Her face contorted and streaked with black tears. I want to comfort her, I want to tell her we're fine and she did fine and look at how fine we are now, but all that comes out of my mouth is the word Mom. Feeble and whispered and dry.

We had nothing. You were so hungry. Crying for *leche*. No one would help us. But he did. He was good to us. Thank Jesus for Father Gafford. Without him, I don't know. I don't know . . .

Now it is real. The memory of my mother with Father Gafford and my hunger and my drinking the turpentine and Dad racing to the hospital and my baby brother dying in a rathole tenement with the monster in the black suit, it's all real in the car. Sitting between us like a cloud of light. It's real and alive in her mascara tears and in her hands still holding back more sobs and in her look, which captures all the terror, hope and gratitude that her life in El Segundo taught her. Not a mural. Not a second-floor walkway. Not a memory. But real.

We cruise back onto Paisano Street and head home. She wipes her eyes with her sleeve and stares blankly out the window. I keep my eyes fixed on the road. Neither of us can muster any more words. It's silence we crave. We don't know why we need this, but we do.

THE WANT

FIRST CHRISTMAS BACK FROM COLLEGE and El Paso is a stark and lonely place. My dad's asleep in his easy chair. Mom's got the *caldo de pollo* simmering on the stove for me. But something else simmers in my private heart. A carnal wanting that grinds me down. An unquiet urge slowly reaming me out.

I'm locked in my room, poring over my high school yearbook, studying the florid signatures of all my pretty classmates beseeching me to call whenever I'm in town. Hearts for punctuation. Smiley faces dotting the i's. 2 Sweet 2 B 4 Got 10 . . . What can they possibly mean except U R 4 Got 10 already?

Dad knocks on the door and asks if I'm okay. I tell him I'm going to see a friend. But it's late, he says. Not late for me. It's 10:30, he says. That's early, I tell him. When they're in bed, I take the keys and go.

The roads are quiet. The sky is overcast. Bing Crosby on the radio wants to make me cry. I follow the city lodestar, there on the Franklin Mountains, the giant five-pointed pentagram of bright electric bulbs that light up every Christmas. I pull into a bar to drink but it's strange sitting by myself with all these older blinder boozers who can hardly finish a sentence, so I leave. I almost hit another bar but the lone drunk with his pecker out is pissing the word "NO" on the wall outside. I don't want a drink. I don't need a drink. I need a girl, some girl to lie to, hold, feel against me, someone to give me a little nighttime CPR, for god's sake. Just one time. One night. That's all.

The loneliness is hurting really bad now. It's not in the

heart but in the head like a migraine shooting icicles into the back of my eyes. It's in my throat too, sore with the whispers that keep hissing out of my mouth like bile. All around me, the streets are barren and shiny in the night. All mortals hidden, out of reach. This is what my born-again high school teacher said would happen. You abandon the Lord and you'll feel the desolation of that choice. You'll be more alone than you could ever imagine. Painful and paralyzing is the sinner's harrowing.

It's about two in the morning. A purgatory of empty streets, at every intersection a population of one. What am I looking for? Who do I hope to see? Maybe this girl, coming down Chelsea Street by the railroads tracks. She's all alone, walking in a coat with a fur collar over a pale dress. We exchange looks as I pass her and I can see that she is a little scared. Not only that. She's pregnant. In spite of how it looks, I have to stop.

I lower the passenger window and wait for her. Are you okay? Do you need a lift home? She replies in her broken English that yes, she wants to go home, but it's a little far. I tell her it's okay, I'm not in any hurry and I have plenty of gas. And with apprehension in her eyes, she steps into my car.

We don't say a word as I pull away and head down Paisano Street. At last, in a tremulous voice, I tell her she shouldn't be out this late. Dangerous for a girl in her condition. She says she was coming from a party but her ride left without her. I hope you didn't drink much, I say. She turns to me with a smile.

Why, you got some?

I don't know what to say. What can I do except shake my head and ask her where she lives so I can take her home? She says we're heading in that direction already. She says something about how pretty the star looks tonight, throwing that glow up into the clouds, and how every Christmas she's always surprised when it's there. *Un milagro*, she calls it. Then she asks me, How come you are out so late *también*?

I want to tell her so much. I want to tell her how something dropped out of me at school one day, some essential cog of faith, and now God means nothing to me, and my night is devoid of people, like they've all gone to some other more rapturous place and left me behind and even my heart has deserted me for being such a traitor to myself and all I have is my body craving something it can't put words to. But all I say is I can't sleep and driving relaxes me. There's a long pause after that and I can feel her smiling again.

Lucky for me, she says.

I tell her that I draw strength from her company and I take it as a propitious sign that she appeared like a mirage after seeing almost nobody for hours.

A sign of what?

I can't answer that. I shrug and ask her how long before her baby comes.

Two months. Maybe sooner.

Wow. That's incredible.

She nods and turns up the Johnny Mathis "Silver Bells."

Are we close, I ask.

She says, Yes. Real close.

Tell me when to stop.

Here.

But there's nothing there. Just a crumbling old sidewalk leading to a small park near the zoo. I pull over anyhow and tell her goodnight and that I hope she . . . but before I finish my words she sidles up to my side and lays her hand right on my crotch and presses down.

What are you doing?

Ándale, papacito. You don't fool me. This is what you want.

Please don't do that.

She moves her face close to mine as she strokes me. You like this, no? You drive all night looking for me. And here I am.

Please don't.

What? I'm not doing nothin'.

But your baby . . .

She snorts. He won't get in the way, she says. *No manches, papacito.* How much do you have?

I'm horrified that this is all my abject misery, my loneliness, has convened for my sake. This pregnant girl. This lewd moment. Held fast in her hand like a gift.

I don't have anything. I don't want this. Please take your hand off.

She does. I shut off the radio and stare at the ridges on the steering wheel.

I didn't know you were . . . I had no idea—

Don't fool yourself. You knew. You knew the whole time. Why did you pick me up?

I don't get it. How can you do this? You're so young and nice-looking and you got a baby on the way.

I got another one at home. Give me twenty dollars *y me voy.*

Twenty dollars?

For my Christmas, *papacito.*

I take out my wallet and give her thirty. When she opens the car door, the overhead light comes on and I see her. She doesn't look sexy or salacious, only poor. Poor and tired and done with cowards like me. With the sort of pride that seems somehow fitting to the moment, she holds up the bills and says, You knew. Then she gets out and walks back in the direction I found her.

Driving back to my house in the hush of the town, I deal with my confusion and my hard-on and the wrenching fires in my heart and come to a realization. Want is not the same as need. I want the girl but she needs the money. Want is her hand on my crotch, need is the baby. The want may be a craving so profound that unfulfilled it can hurt like death, but the need is life itself. The want made me roam all over like a rutting animal but the need will take me home. And how fucking

Catholic of me, to pick up Mother Mary on a Christmas night and wind up with a prostitute in her third trimester. What a fucking cliché. But maybe it takes a cliché to slap me across the face with the ironies that make El Paso the raw-boned place it is. God doesn't have to live here, but people do. We try, anyway. The hard-bitten wants and needs of our lives blur into something wondrous and terrible, beyond reality, beyond reproach, our own dirty human miracle like the electric star of Bethlehem blinking off in the gauzy haze of dawn.

THE RUNNER II

I ARRIVE WITH MY GIRLFRIEND to introduce her to my parents because I intend to marry her within a year or so. But the sight of my old town shames me. So washed-out, ragged and sere. Smelling of that refinery funk. And worse, our old house. Small and simple and the yard pocked with large patches of dead ryegrass and my parents are humble and uncomplicated in their way, and I'm afraid she'll find them perhaps somewhat below the educational level of the people she and I mingle with. But once they get to know her and she them, there is instant rapport, the laughter between them easy and warm. They're darling, she says. They're smart and wise, she says. So there it is.

I am sent out to buy refreshments for the dinner to come. I drive along Alameda Street toward the *mercado*. The sun still searing in its mountain cradle. There I see him, running on a narrow strip of desert earth along the road, right beside the car. He's a local fixture by now, which is ironic because there's nothing fixed about him. His clothes are threadbare and dirty like a mendicant's and his scaly bare arms flail in the air as he runs. His hair is a tangled mane of long strands of matted filth running down his back. I slow down to get a closer look. On a stubbled face scalded by sun and wind, his eyes, unfocused and milky, seem to regard nothing but the ground in front. There is sweat streaming down his neck, dried snot on his cheek. He's a little older than I am, maybe older than that. What terrors keep him on this crazy treadmill? What scared him so badly that he's still running for cover? Who left this poor straggler behind, abandoned him to this perpetual marathon, this race without a tape? I remember the Tarahumara Indians and their almost superhuman proclivity for running long distances, who repulsed the Spanish church and colonists for generations, and I wonder if this runner is searching for his tribe. I steady the car even with him, but he quickens his pace. He's clearly running from something now. He wants none of my scrutiny. I think he's done with all that. Outran our judgments many miles ago.

Without turning his head, I feel his eyes blur in my direction for an instant. This is my city, they seem to say. I run and run but here I am. Where are *you*? What are *you* running from? Who left *you* behind? The prodigal bitch is *you*. It is then I see that pride and shame are the same sin. One diminishes my family and the life they gave me, the other diminishes me. The last harsh rays of day gather on the glass as I let him dash between moving cars across the intersection. A blur sidestepping all my lame suppositions. Running. Running. *Indio como yo.*

NETO

I HAVE A BROTHER WHO died before he reached his first birthday. I think I ran into him at the airport. I'm waiting this one afternoon for a flight at El Paso International that keeps getting delayed every hour. I sit and put on my earbuds and listen to a random selection of electronica, jazz, maybe something ambient. There's a point where the sounds in your head synchronize with eye focus and everything drops into a general blur. I zone out like that for a minute when gradually I sense him sitting across from me. My brother. I know it's him because he looks like me, only a year younger. Less grey in his hair, fewer wrinkles around the mouth. Sleepy self-assured eyes. A face that don't give a shit. I never really liked the phrase "comfortable in his skin" because I've never been comfortable in mine. But he is: the way he sits, the way his work boots sprawl toward me. I have my sunglasses on, which is how I size him up without him knowing.

I notice a silver cross around his neck, the kind that is both tribal and religious. There are four or five tiny black tats on his hands, and though I can't see it under his clothes, I suspect he wears the Guadalupe Virgin over his heart. I can tell by the gentle curl of his lips that they're more accustomed to speaking Spanish than English. He has his own inaudible music playing in his head and judging by the cadence in his nod, I guess it's the *boleros* of my mom's old records. He is all the Mexican I have tried to be but can't.

Then in that languorous haze I see into his heavy-lidded eyes and his essential nature lays itself bare. I'm a Sunday man, he says inside, I kneel when the Father says to. I love my women. I sin against them and never apologize for it, except by loving them more. I know all the ways of loneliness, and all the ways to nurse it. I'm a nightbird, my eyes attuned to the nuances of dark, and it's in that place I hide my saddest dreams, my delirious vices. Pain is grace. I don't know how not to do something, only that not doing it brings more regret than I can bear. Trouble's bitten me so many times, it's left black marks on my hands, marks that commemorate loss and love and maybe an unborn child or two. I've seen death more than most, so count on me to be present at your last rites. That's how our blood must have it. I am lived-in, a lived-in man. Your *carnal.* Your bro.

He cuts me a single glance that lasts as long as it takes to say his name and his look says, 'Cause I'm dead, I got permission to fuck my life up and still outlive you. A woman's voice says something over the intercom and he gets up and walks to his gate. And I get up and walk to mine.

MY RIGHT FOOT

I SEE IT ON MY way out to the airport. The largest equestrian statue in the world, Don Juan de Oñate on his rearing stallion looking larger than even the jet planes that circle over him. *El conquistador español* who founded our city. Fuck. He's the Big Bad Daddy of the town, as omnipresent as the sun, which cuts a deep shadow from his visored helmet over his bronzed eyes. That shadow is his darker legacy of murder and brutality that we're still living down today. Like the blueprint for our future scrolled up neatly in his hand. Oñate and his men put down a rebellion of the Acoma Pueblo Indians in New Mexico, killing 600 of them, and then ordered that all surviving males over twenty-five have their right feet severed clean off just to make sure they stay put. That was in 1598, but it seems like everywhere I look, people are still hobbling around, walking the slow hulking walk of the lifelong cripple. Maybe that's why so many of us hardly ever stray far from the city limits. We loiter around our personal ruined memories like ghosts. Like that mute runner with the long hair dashing along Alameda as if in terror of Oñate chasing his ass down. Or those rumbling sedans with puffy-eyed low-res *vatos* cruising the parks and *callejones* with their Jack Daniels in paper bags and blunts in the ashtray, looking for God knows what in the middle of the night. Maybe their own chopped-off feet.

At the TSA screening, I look down at my Tony Lamas as I take them off and watch them disappear into the X-ray machine, and I think of a *retablo* of a bloody pile of right feet with the Holy Virgin suspended above them, I think of how

I've been lamed by my own past and then I think of how often I've walked away and yet always manage to walk back. We'd all like to shed our dimmest and most painful memories, to disown them or reimagine them as miracles of restitution, circles of renewal. Sometimes they are. But I'm late for my flight and Oñate's on his unblinkered horse, almost airborne, hooves raised, hooves high, hooves reaching for the deadpan skies of *el paso del norte*.

THE RUNNER III

I SEE HIM ONE MORE time.

Driving through New Mexico on a cold bright January day. Only a few more miles to the city limits, to the place I used to call home. I have to take a piss. I pull over to a truck stop, tank up, relieve myself and buy a candy bar for the road. On the way to the car, the sprinting man is there.

He's old. His clothes fused to his body, all gray as cement. His beard gray too. His eyes sunken into a face long and drawn and darker than I remember. His ancient tennis shoes are missing their laces and there are no socks. Dark sweat stains on his shirt and on the seat of his pants. The veins on his arms and his neck are thick and ropey and I picture all his frame strung together with rebar. Like a statue, which is ironic, 'cause there's nothing statuesque about him. He's still racing as hard and fast as his legs will take him, though he's hardly a blur by now.

But maybe he is. 'Cause nobody sees him. Nobody sees the prints he leaves behind on the coarse gravel shoulder. Nobody hears the wheeze of his breathing. Nobody seems to be aware of the displacement of air along that part of the frontage road. It's like he's moving in time to the Earth's rotation, as fast as the clouds' progress in the bleak sky above. I wonder if he's been running in place the whole time. Catching up with his life, which apparently remains just out of arm's reach. I know he has to have stopped somewhere, for sleep, for food, for the evacuation of his bowels. For love and companionship. And there must have been a place and time when he didn't run, where being stationary made all the sense in the world. I think I'm trying to say the word home. When he stops, when he finally takes no more strides and comes to a complete halt, maybe that's where he'll be. Maybe that's where he's going.

I get in my car and drive in the opposite direction. I'm watching him the whole time in my rear-view mirror as we head toward our horizons, him to his vanishing point and me to mine.

Author of more than twenty plays, **Octavio Solis** is considered one of the most prominent Latino playwrights in America. His works have been produced in theatres across the country, including the Center Group Theatre and the Mark Taper Forum in Los Angeles, South Coast Repertory, the Magic Theatre and the California Shakespeare Theatre in the San Francisco Bay Area, Yale Repertory Theatre, Oregon Shakespeare Festival, Dallas Theater Center, and other venues nationwide. Among his many awards and grants, Solis has received an NEA Playwriting Fellowship, the Kennedy Center's Roger L. Stevens Award, the TCG/NEA Theatre Artists in Residence Grant, the National Latino Playwriting Award, and the PEN Center USA Award for Drama.

His fiction and short plays have appeared in the *Louisville Review, Zyzzyva, Eleven Eleven, Catamaran, Chicago Quarterly Review, Arroyo Literary Review* and *Huizache*. This is his first book.

For more information: www.octaviosolis.net

ACKNOWLEDGMENTS

I would like to acknowledge the following for inspiring and supporting the work of these Retablos throughout their various stages of development: Oscar Villalon and Laura Cogan of *Zyzzyva*, Elizabeth McKenzie, Catherine Segurson and Chorel R. Centers of *Catamaran*, Jenn Bennet of *Arroyo Literary Review*, Dagoberto Gilb and *Huizache*, Peter Maravelis, Stacey Lewis, and my scrupulous editor Elaine Katzenberger of City Lights Books, Charlie Jane Anders of Writers with Drinks, Word for Word Performing Arts Company, Frances Lefkowitz, Amanda Moody, and Karen Macklin. None of this would be possible without my daughter Gracie and my dear wife Jeanne, who with her unerring love and counsel helped me navigate the faulty shoals of memory and invention. But to the family represented in these pages, I owe so much more.